Making Money the Old-Fashioned Way

– A Story of Black Entrepreneurship –

by - Aaron Bocage and George Waters

*To our parents, George and Victoria Waters, and Sterling and Thelma Bocage,
who taught us long ago the value of hard work and free enterprise.*

ACKNOWLEDGMENTS

To Elizabeth Wright, for her thorough research and excellent writing and for her unwavering support on this project. And for her lifetime commitment to educating the African American community in the challenges and benefits of full participation in the free-market economy.

To Samuel Byrd, for original artwork used in this text.

To the Dover Pictorial Archives Series for supplemental artwork; pages 16, 18, and 38.

To William Campbell, for his valued assistance in the production and editing of this project.

EDTEC®

Education, Training and Enterprise Center, Inc.

Making Money the Old-Fashioned Way

© 1997 EDTEC, Inc.

Published by EDTEC, Inc.
313 Market Street
Camden, NJ 08102
Phone: 1-800-963-9361   Fax: 609-963-8110
World Wide Web Address: http://www.edtecinc.com

See the back of this book for additional titles available through EDTEC, Inc.

51395

9 780966 171204

Printed in the United States of America

Table of Contents

Introduction

MAKING MONEY THE OLD-FASHIONED WAY
From Slavery to Prosperity

Entrepreneurship in the black community is not a brand-new concept. It is an idea that African Americans have been developing for centuries. The history of blacks in America is an inspiring story of ingenuity and invention in the face of adversity. Long before slavery ended, black Americans engaged in businesses of their own. Their success shaped the course of our nation's history . . . and built a proud tradition for future generations to follow.

We realize that our future lies chiefly in our own hands. We know that neither institution nor friends can make a race stand unless it has strength in its own foundation; that races, like individuals, must stand or fall by their own merit; that to fully succeed they must practice the virtues of self-reliance, self-respect, industry, perseverance, and economy.

— Paul Robeson

.........From Slavery to Economic Champions

As descendants of slaves, African Americans share a legacy of leg irons, broken families, inhuman treatment, and lynchings. Yet in spite of this horrendous past, many African Americans have managed to beat the odds and achieve a level of economic success that many had believed to be impossible.

.........From Slavery to Builder of a $34 Million Rap Empire

As CEO and owner of Rush Communications, Russell Simmons has gone beyond managing artists. Today his company includes seven record labels, several management companies, a film and television division, and a radio production company. Simmons is definitely getting paid.

.........From Slavery to NBA Franchise Owner

For 10 years, Ervin "Magic" Johnson dazzled fans as a superstar basketball player for the LA Lakers. Now Magic has traded playing for the Lakers with being a part owner. With a $10 million investment, Magic now owns 5 percent of the NBA basketball franchise.

.........From Slavery to Having the Largest Media Production Company Ever Owned by an African American Woman

Oprah Winfrey has jumped to superstar status with hard work, determination, and excellent business skills. As the owner of HARPO (Oprah spelled backwards) Productions, Oprah has made a mark in the entertainment industry few can match. With her national talk show, along with production and distribution operations worldwide, Oprah brought in over $175 million in revenue in 1996.

The Common Thread

Aside from their hard work, personal sacrifice, and a refusal to quit, these champions of free enterprise have one element in common: their desire to succeed – which had a far greater impact on them than any obstacles they may have encountered. And while these individuals have surmounted the odds and created opportunities for themselves and others, they are not the only ones. In this book, we shall meet other African Americans who succeeded in spite of overwhelming odds. For now, though, let's take a look at the history of blacks in this country to see just how far they have gone.

A Historical View

The history of black entrepreneurship in this country can be traced to a time before there was an America. Many of the accomplishments of blacks in this country have gone unnoticed by students both black and white. However, the impact of black business enterprise on this country is as strong as the domination of the hip-hop popular culture by black musicians, a few of whom are entrepreneurs themselves.

To see how blacks became entrepreneurs, we must first learn what an entrepreneur is and what factors led people to pursue entrepreneurship as a career.

Our nettlesome task is to discover how to organize our strength into compelling power.

– Martin Luther King, Jr.

The dictionary defines an entrepreneur as one who organizes, operates, and assumes the risk in a business venture in expectation of making a profit.

Farming Outside the United States

On Europe, Africa, and Asia, agriculture, or farming the land, was the main occupation for most people for thousands of years. Before useful tools were invented, farming the land was a long and slow process. People spent many hours in the fields every day to produce just enough food for their families. If a family didn't own the land, they had to pay a share of their crops as rent to the owner of the land, which meant spending more time in the fields.

One of the biggest problems farmers faced was to produce the most food as efficiently as possible. It's a little like Ben, who always complained about having to sort his clothes before he washed them. Ben spent a lot of time separating the dark from the light clothes after they had already been thrown into the hamper. One day during one of his more creative moments, he thought of how to make a tough job a whole lot easier. Ben bought three plastic containers and put them in his room. In one container he threw his jeans, sweat pants, and other dark items. In another container he put his light clothes. In the third container, he put his fine washables, such as his Tommy Hilfiger and Guess shirts.

As a result of his "invention," Ben was able to do the laundry without taking the extra time to separate the items. What a brilliant idea, he thought. Now he had more time to work on his basketball game. Unfortunately, Ben's father had something else in mind, like

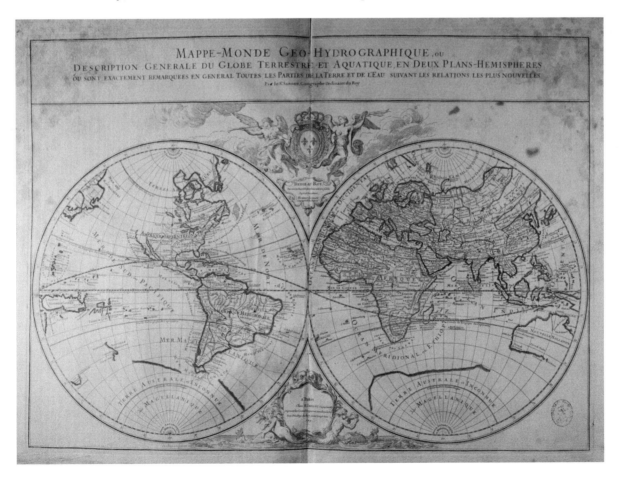

homework. Just as Ben figured out a way to wash clothes more efficiently, early farmers sought ways to develop more efficient tools for farming and learned how to make better use of their farm animals.

The invention that changed the nature of farming and allowed further agricultural inventions was the heavy wheeled plow. This tool made it possible to break and turn heavy soil. As more tools were developed, two things happened:

1. Farmers could produce more food, and

2. They could work more efficiently.

As a result, fewer people were needed to do the work, giving rise to a new economic class. The newly formed merchant class consisted of individuals who continued the spirit of entrepreneurship by seeking better and faster ways of producing and selling goods.

It wasn't long before people in Europe began buying and selling merchandise to other countries that sometimes were thousands of miles away. Individual merchants brought their money together to form joint-stock companies. These companies built and sponsored ships and crews in order to trade goods with countries in the Far East and to search for natural resources in the new world of America. These ships eventually brought the first European settlers to America.

Virginia's first successful colony, Jamestown, was established in 1607 by a commercial trading company.

PRINCIPLE 1: Entrepreneurs constantly look for ways to do jobs easier, faster, and more efficiently.

The Impact of Inventions on Farming

Although some European rulers and enterprising merchants looked to benefit from developing America's natural resources, many of them were attempting to improve life right at home. In England especially, a steady flow of creative ideas resulted in the birth of one invention after another. Beginning around the early 1700s and continuing 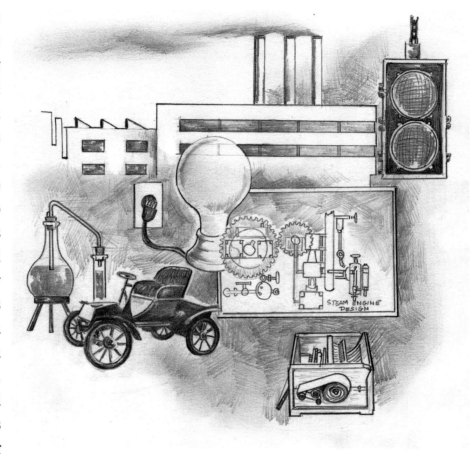 throughout the 19th century, hundreds of ingenious devices were invented. Part of the labor-saving process involved finding innovative solutions to old problems. While this sometimes resulted in the creation of a product, more often than not, someone modified an existing product and found a new application for it.

An example of how several inventors working separately (and even generations apart) can create and modify the same invention is the steam engine. This machine was to become the driving force that operated other machinery. Before the steam engine was invented in England, laborers who manufactured goods in workshops had to depend upon windmills, watermills, draft animals, and their own strength for power to operate machinery. Over several years, Thomas Savery, Thomas Newcomen, and James Watt, working separately, used their knowledge of science and mechanics to come up with a machine that would reduce the need for physical labor. The result of their collective genius was the steam engine.

In 1698, Savery turned his attention to solving a serious problem that troubled coal miners. The miners faced danger from the flooding of deep mines, and work was slowed whenever a mine was flooded. Workers had to stop to pump the water out of the mines by hand. Savery designed an engine that condensed steam in a vessel and created a vacuum into which water was forced by atmospheric pressure.

In 1712, Newcomen improved on Savery's invention by adding a piston to a cylinder. This made the machine work even more efficiently and kept mines free of water. But it was James Watt who would make what is still considered the most crucial modification to the steam engine. Almost 50 years after Newcomen's invention, Watt created a mechanism that converted the back-and-forth motion of the piston into a steady rotary motion. This made it possible for the steam engine to be the prime mover for all kinds of other machinery. The steam engine made other sources of power like watermills and windmills operate faster and more consistently.

PRINCIPLE 2:
Entrepreneurs find ways to make existing products work even better.

We mentioned that the steam engine was developed through the efforts of several inventors. What we didn't say was that one of those inventors was a black man named Elijah McCoy. McCoy picked up where Newcomen left off by designing the lubricator cup. The rotary motion of the steam engine, made possible by Newcomen, created heat friction that damaged the moving parts of the steam engine. In 1872 McCoy solved this problem by creating a lubricator cup for steam engines. This enabled machines to be oiled while in motion.

McCoy's parents, who had been slaves in Kentucky, fled to Canada, to raise their children in freedom. McCoy was born in Ontario in 1843. As a boy, he became interested in engineering. After completing high school, he apprenticed as a mechanical engineer. He later moved to Detroit and took a job as a fireman on the Michigan Central Railroad because as a black man, he couldn't find a job in his field. While he worked for the railroad, one of his duties was to keep the train's steam engine oiled, a job he regularly performed after first shutting down the engine. The exhausting job of oiling the engine by hand was necessary in order to prevent heat friction from wearing out and destroying the engine's parts. This time-consuming process caused delays in the train's schedule and was most inefficient.

In the spirit of a true inventor, McCoy was determined to develop a new method for lubricating the engine. After much experimentation, he perfected a lubricator cup that could effectively oil an engine while it was still running. His patented invention became mandatory equipment because gears and moving parts of locomotives and heavy machinery could be continuously lubricated without stopping the engines. Over the years, McCoy patented several more lubricators that he designed for other types of machinery.

Because the steam engine was a key component in operating other types of machinery, it would become the cornerstone invention for the mechanized factory system. For the first time, machinery could be powered by using coal, oil, and natural gas instead of employing animals, windmills, or human labor. The steam engine provided power for textile factories, iron foundries, and flour mills. But, more important, the steam engine was the key to the creation of new industries.

Inventions and the Free Market

As the factory system of manufacturing became widespread, work was gradually reorganized. Where family members might be employed by an entrepreneur to sew or craft merchandise in their home, they were now replaced by machines that performed those same tasks more quickly and cheaply. For example, instead of the entrepreneur's receiving only 10 or 20 items from his home workers in the course of a day or a week, it was now possible to produce hundreds of items in the same amount of time in a factory.

As the nature of work changed, so did the social conditions. People who once worked on farms moved to the manufacturing centers in order to work in factories. Small communities grew into moderate-sized towns and towns expanded into cities.

The steam engine was applied throughout all industrial segments of society, including mining, transportation, manufacturing, and even printing. In each case, the steam engine transformed that industry and made it possible to satisfy the needs and demands of masses of people.

Right behind the steam engine came a new chemical process that could convert pig iron into steel. Because of this invention, it became possible to produce steel cheaply and more reliably. As we shall see in Chapter 4, cheaply produced steel led to the development of the railroad, the steamship, and thousands of other items that had been made primarily from wood.

The development of the steam engine gives one a glimpse of the free market at work. As machinery was able to produce more goods, people demanded more. This leads to another principle of business.

PRINCIPLE 3: Supply must keep up with demand.

This demand created the incentive for inventors and entrepreneurs to work at finding better ways to produce goods faster and more efficiently to satisfy the market. They were rewarded for their innovation through the buying and selling of goods and they were very eager to keep their new, but profitable, businesses going. Historians refer to the huge economic and social changes brought on by these inventions as a revolution. It is common to speak of an Agricultural Revolution and an Industrial Revolution. The term revolution is applied to these events because the societies affected were never the same again.

If there is no struggle, there is no progress. Those who profess to favor freedom, and yet deprecate agitation, are men who want crops without plowing up the ground. They want the ocean without the awful roar of its many waters. This struggle may be a moral one; or it may be a physical one; or it may be both moral and physical; but it must be a struggle. Power concedes nothing without a demand.

— Frederick Douglass

Life Back Home

On the American continent and years before the technologic advances (discussed in Chapter 1), life was still at a pre-industrial stage when those who settled the Jamestown colony in Virginia realized that they were not prepared for the harshness of life they were to experience. About half of them starved to death during the first two years. Their attempts to cultivate crops that were common to Europe failed, because such crops could not thrive in the rich American soil. Wheat, a hardy staple in England, could not be cultivated in Virginia or in the North, where the Pilgrims settled a decade later.

The surviving settlers had to adapt to a whole new set of circumstances and they had to learn to do this from the native people who were most familiar with the weather and soil conditions. From the Indians, the settlers learned to cultivate sweet potatoes, squash, pumpkins, watermelon, and especially corn. Corn became the great food staple for all the colonies because flour made from corn could be used in a variety of foods. Corn could also be made into an excellent feed for livestock.

The settlers' methods of farming, though, were far more advanced than those of the Indians. Back in England, farmers had pretty much perfected farming techniques and had become proficient in using farm implements. They adapted these tools to their new environment. Using the shovels, spades, sickles, and scythes to work the land gave them a great advantage. Unlike in England, however, the only domestic animal in America was the dog. The colonists sorely missed the draft animals that had eased their labor back in England. This, along with the constant uncertainties they faced in the new land, made them just a little homesick. To make matters worse, it was years before they were financially able to import horses and livestock, such as sheep, cattle, chickens, and pigs, from Europe. As soon as they were able to, they also imported plows from Europe, which increased their work output tremendously.

For the merchants who had sponsored the first settlers, though, the Virginia colony was a failure. The surviving settlers struggled to scrape out a living and were desperate to buy products and tools from Europe which they could not manufacture in America.

In 1612, one of the colonists who was a farmer planted tobacco, a commodity he was familiar with because he had smoked it in the old country. Years before the settlers sailed to America, sailors had introduced tobacco to England. The crop had been cultivated by slaves in the Spanish colonies of the Caribbean for at least a century before the Pilgrims landed in the New World.

Tobacco turned out to be the crop that would save the Virginia colonists. It was highly desired in England and other parts of Europe, and it grew with ease in the fertile river valleys of the American South. Virginia's many rivers allowed ships to penetrate inland to plantation wharves, where the tobacco was loaded. Tobacco and eventually rice, indigo, furs, and lumber eliminated economic anxiety for many settlers because they were successfully traded abroad for manufactured goods.

PRINCIPLE 4:

Entrepreneurs can sometimes take advantage of unplanned events in the social or economic arena. For example, when mothers returned to the work force in huge numbers during the early 1970s, entrepreneurs took advantage of the need for child care by providing day-care centers. Merchants, likewise, took advantage of the availability of tobacco by selling it to Europeans.

Early Settlers Used Natural Resources for Business Opportunities

In the 17th and 18th centuries, the fur trade greatly influenced colonial life. Thousands in the colonies were able to raise their standard of living, because of the insatiable demand in Europe for pelts that could be manufactured into coats and other popular items. In the northern colonies, the English fur trade was centered in the Hudson Bay region of New York State. Alliances with Indian tribes, such as the Iroquois, were essential to the trapping of animals. A cooperative chain was established between settlers and Indians that brought furs from forest to storehouse and from there to the boats bound for Europe. In the South, Charleston, South Carolina, and Augusta, Georgia, were the major points in fur trading. Ships sailed abroad from the port of Charleston. In this region, agreements were made with the Cherokee Indians.

Like fur, timber resources seemed inexhaustible. The pine tree was especially prized, not only because its wood could be easily crafted, but because it also provided tar. Oak trees provided potash, which was widely used in making soap and in glassmaking. The manufacture of soap and glass required only an iron pot or a small kiln, which made these occupations ideal for those living in a nontechnological society. Many families throughout the colonies earned their livelihoods working at these trades.

The seas also were explored for resources. One of the world's finest fishing grounds stretched from the tip of New York's Long Island northward to Canada's Newfoundland. There was a ready market abroad, as well as in the colonies, for dried codfish, mackerel, bass, and herring. This new industry kept thousands of fishermen working a variety of jobs in the fisheries.

Although great numbers of people earned a living from the fur, lumber, and fishing industries, the overwhelming majority of colonists continued to work at farming. Agriculture was still the primary means of day-to-day survival.

PRINCIPLE 5:

Entrepreneurs often establish agreements with others who control the resources they need to sell their goods. This principle is exemplified by recording artists who cut deals with record stores or other distribution outlets that can get the records to the consumers. The early settlers did something similar with the Indians. Since the Indians controlled the land needed to get through to the shipping zones, the settlers made agreements (alliances) with the Indians.

People Settled in the New World for Different Reasons

• To Escape Religious Persecution

The Europeans who first settled the colonies of the New World came for different reasons. Some came because they were escaping persecution for their religious beliefs. The earliest of these settlers were the various sects of Puritans who settled in Plymouth and Salem in Massachusetts.

• To Look for Gold

Other settlements were initiated by businessmen, some of whom expected to find gold or other precious metals. Unfortunately, such resources did not exist on the eastern coast of the American continent.

• To Rent Out Land

In other instances, a company or a wealthy nobleman would sponsor a group of people to settle a particular region, expecting the settlers to pay rent for the land they would farm. However, once the settlers arrived in America, they found it difficult to live up to such arrangements and wanted to own their farms outright. After some squabbling and attempts at legal action, many European sponsors gave in to these rebellious settlers. In some cases, contracts were renegotiated and farmers were given the right to buy land in the settlement. They did so, however, with the understanding that they would turn over a certain amount of their harvest each year to the sponsoring company or nobleman.

These farmers were the fortunate people. They were among those who had voluntarily emigrated from Europe. There were many other Europeans who came to America against their will.

• To Serve as Forced Indentured Servants

Criminals who were given the choice of prison in the old country or forced servitude in the new chose to serve out their prison sentences as unpaid laborers in the colonies. Such sentences could last for several years, or until the prisoners died.

Another group of settlers were those who had been arrested back in England for debts they owed either to merchants, landlords, banks, or money lenders. Throughout Europe, unpaid debt was a serious offense, and it was common to find debtors' prisons filled with people who had been reduced to poverty. Such debtors were allowed to indenture themselves as unpaid laborers in order to work off their debts. Thousands of such people came to work in America, where newly established plantations were creating a pressing need for labor. This type of indenture could last anywhere from five to ten years.

Each of us has the right and the responsibility to assess the roads which lie ahead and . . . if the future road looms ominous or unpromising . . . then we need to gather our resolve and . . . step off . . . into another direction.

– Maya Angelou

• To Serve as Voluntary Indentured Servants

Still others who wanted to start life over in the New World, but could not afford the cost of passage or the price of a piece of farmland, voluntarily indentured themselves to others for a specified number of years. Occasionally the terms of a contract would specify that a tract of land be given to the indentured worker once the period of labor was fulfilled.

• To Serve as Slaves

Next came the most unfortunate group of settlers. They were Europeans who were literally kidnapped and sold into slavery. Usually, these individuals were orphans or the children of paupers. They were captured by gangs and sold to ship captains, who then resold them into chattel slavery in the New World. (The word kidnapper is defined in early English dictionaries as "A stealer of human beings, especially of children, originally for exportation to the plantations of North America.") Vast numbers of white Europeans served as slaves in the colonies before and during the importation and enslavement of Africans.

All Settlers Had a Link to Business

Though there were many types of people who settled in America for various reasons, the bond they all shared was their connection in some way to business.

The settlers who escaped religious persecution came to the New World and immediately began to farm the land. They often traded food with the Indians in exchange for goods that they could not produce themselves. This practice is referred to as bartering, the act of trading goods or services without the use of money. In the case of those sent to America by European businessmen, the settlers' mission was to find gold and other precious materials that could be sold in Europe for a profit. Those sent to farm the land and pay rent found themselves in a business arrangement by agreeing to give their sponsors a portion of their harvest even after they had purchased the land. Those who worked the farms to settle debt obligations provided free labor. This meant that whatever food items were produced from their toil could be sold at 100 percent profit because there was no labor charge.

Slavery's Influence on Black Entrepreneurship

Throughout the ages, humans have enslaved one another. Sometimes wars were begun for the main purpose of capturing people to enslave. At other times, battles fought for other reasons resulted in the taking of prisoners, who then became valuable booty to be sold in slave markets. Some rulers regularly went on hunts to capture boys and men in order to provide soldiers for their armies.

The best-known slave-owning societies are those of

Greece in the 5th through 3rd centuries BC, and

Rome in the 2nd century BC through 4th century AD.

There were many societies that bought, sold, and traded slaves. Europe's Crimean Tatars, for example, regularly raided their Slavic neighbors, captured them, and sold them into slavery throughout the known world. (The word slave comes from a reference to the Slavic people of Europe.)

By the 1300s, the Ottoman Empire (Turkey) was a major slave trader. Millions of captives from the white Slavic north and from the black African south flowed through its slave markets. This occurred over many generations.

In Africa, slave societies were common. Slavery existed in Ghana and Mali long before Europeans began trading African slaves. The Kingdom of Dahomey was particularly notorious for slave-trading. By the 1800s, many societies existed where about half of the population were slaves.

This was true for the

 **Ashanti**

 **Yoruba, and**

 **Ibo peoples, as well as those in**

 **Dahomey and Sierra Leone on the continent of Africa.**

Slavery in the American Colonies

As the southern plantation system expanded in the American colonies and consumer demand for tobacco and cotton products increased at home and abroad, the supply of labor could not keep up with the demand. Earlier attempts to force the native Indians into labor had failed, and it became harder to induce European workers to come to the New World once the harsh conditions of plantation labor became known to them. In a region like the South, which had a long growing season, a laborer could expect to work the full 200 to 290 hot days per year. Such a prospect was not inviting to those who might voluntarily migrate from Europe. By the mid-1700s, it had become less feasible to kidnap and enslave Europeans, a great many of whom bolted from such forced labor and blended in with the country's majority white population.

I, young in life, by seeming cruel fate ... Was snatch'd from Afric's fancy'd happy seat.

– Phillis Wheatley

For the African, the great misfortune was not only that there was a ready market for his labor, but that there existed a sophisticated network of slave traders throughout Africa. This system, which had been going on for centuries, was established by Africans themselves, some of whom were powerful tribal chiefs. To these traders, the American continent became just another market in which they continued the long tradition of selling human beings.

The first Africans arrived in Virginia in 1619 and their numbers increased as crops, such as cotton and tobacco, were vigorously exported to the markets of Europe and Asia. By 1700, African slavery was firmly established in the South. Although the majority of slaves were first engaged as agricultural workers, either on plantations or on other types of farms, vast numbers were employed in other occupations.

Not All Slaves Were Treated the Same

When most people think of American slavery, they think of plantations and field hands. While this depiction is accurate, tens of thousands of skilled slaves were hired out by their owners to work for others. In addition to the typical plantation owner, there were southerners who were business proprietors or craftsmen. Such people, if they owned slaves at all, usually owned no more than one or two. If an owner was a builder of houses, for example, his slaves learned construction and built houses. If he was a carpenter, they learned carpentry. Or an owner might apprentice his slave or slaves to a craftsman to learn a particular skill so they could be hired out as workers. The average white southerner who might have had a small farm did not own slaves at all.

Because of their training in trades, millions of black men and women developed skills that were to benefit them and their families long after slavery ended. In general, slaves were viewed as valuable investments. Although the institution of slavery should never be condoned in any sense, the treatment of slaves differed according to local social customs

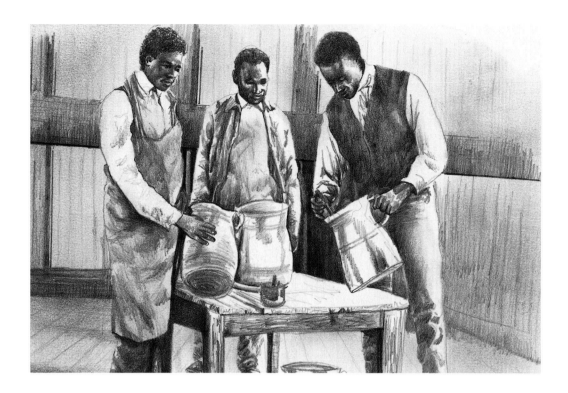

and the attitudes of individual slave owners. In New Orleans, for example, depending on the nature of the work required of them, some slaves had a remarkable degree of personal freedom to come and go, similar to that of white citizens.

From its earliest introduction into America, slavery was looked down upon by a great many whites, who expressed moral outrage and opposition to the enslavement of human beings. In the early 19th century, a Virginian expressed his aversion by describing slavery as a "cruel and shameful enterprise managed by the depraved and greedy." Even then, there were whites who noted the contradiction between the noble sentiments concerning individual liberty by America's founders and the blatant denial of liberty to a whole population.

Years before the Civil War, some southerners made attempts to end slavery. Besides the organized abolitionist groups, consisting of northerners and southerners, there were thousands of other people who lent their efforts to bring slavery to an end. As the economies of different regions changed, many people opposed slavery for practical reasons because they believed it to be an unprofitable enterprise. In 1832, a bill that would have speeded up the process of emancipating slaves was defeated by only one vote in the Virginia assembly.

Slaves' Participation in the Free Enterprise System

From the first years of American slavery, there were numbers of slaves who were set free. Therefore, throughout the slavery period, until the issuance of the Emancipation Proclamation in 1863, a population of free blacks existed right along with those who were in bondage.

There were several reasons a slave might be set free. For example:

- **An owner may have died and the heirs may not have wished to own slaves.**

- **A person who opposed slavery bought slaves in order to free them.**

- **Whites formed groups just for the purpose of leading slaves to freedom.**

- **A slave was freed as a reward for his good service to the owner.**

- **When permitted, slaves worked their way out of slavery, freeing themselves and family members.**

Frank McWhorter was a slave who lived from 1777 to 1854 and was allowed to run his own business, as long as he gave a certain percentage of his earnings to his owner. He established a plant where he produced saltpeter, a substance used in fertilizer and as a main ingredient of gunpowder. With profits from his business, McWhorter bought his own freedom and that of 16 family members. Such a slave was known to "hire his own time." McWhorter went on, in 1836, to found the town of New Philadelphia in Illinois, where he operated other businesses.

Another slave, John Berry Meachum, in the early 1800s, was allowed to establish a carpentry business. From his earnings, he bought his freedom and that of his family and 20 nonrelatives. After moving to St. Louis, Missouri, Meachum established several small businesses and also built two commercial steamboats for cruising the Mississippi.

The color of the skin is no way connected with the strength of the mind or intellectual powers.

– Benjamin Banneker

In 1794, in Nashville, Tennessee, Robert Rentfro was allowed to sell food and liquor. By 1801, he was able to purchase his own freedom. He bought a plot of land from his former owner and established what became a popular inn and livery stable.

These men represent thousands more who made the best of the bad deal of slavery. As we will see in Chapter 4, American blacks were fired by the spirit of enterprise and invention that seized Americans of all backgrounds. As skilled craftsmen and entrepreneurs, they contributed to the newly developing nation. The absence of political freedom during the slavery period did not stop free blacks from becoming successful entrepreneurs and landowners. Despite racial bigotry, they proved themselves to be skilled artisans and farmers. This was possible because of the underlying principle that prevailed among Americans, the individual's right to own property. This notion of the sanctity of private property protected the landowner, whether foreigner, citizen, or slave. It was this principle that made it possible for a great many blacks to prosper and thrive even during the darkest days of slavery.

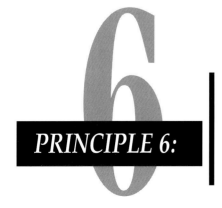

PRINCIPLE 6:

The desire of entrepreneurs to succeed is stronger than the limitations they often encounter. This was the case with the slaves who became businessmen in spite of slavery.

25

The Seeds of American Entrepreneurship

Throughout the colonial period in America, it was the farmer, not the businessman, who was the average American citizen. The new technology that mechanized England's factory system was unknown in the colonies, where most of the production was still being done manually.

From 1776, with the Declaration of Independence, until the last battle of the Revolution in 1781, the colonies were busy trying to break political ties to Britain. However, Americans were still very dependent upon Britain economically, especially for manufactured products. Machine-spun cotton, for example, was much cheaper and of better quality than most of what was hand spun.

Be not discouraged. There is a future for you ... The resistance encountered now predicates hope ... Only as we rise ... do we encounter opposition.

— **Frederick Douglass**

Throughout the period of the Revolution and for years afterwards, Britain did all it could to prevent the export of machinery that had made its factory system the greatest in the world and had given the country a monopoly in many markets. The British government placed restrictions on blueprints and plans of machinery and even forbade certain workers who were familiar with machine designs from leaving the country.

Needless to say, these restrictions were not effective for long. Eventually, various plans were smuggled out of the country by businessmen and skilled mechanics. Samuel Slater, born in England and a trained mechanic, memorized the plans for spinning machinery and slipped out of the country in 1789. In 1790, in Rhode Island, he built his own spinning machine to make cotton thread, and the first American factory was born.

Mechanization and Invention Change America

Slater's success led him to open several more plants. As others learned from him, they branched out and founded their own small factories. This factory system, which specialized in the manufacture of cloth, spread to Massachusetts, where Francis Lowell established several large factories between 1813 and 1850. Lowell was among the first American entrepreneurs to combine large-scale operation with professional management and marketing procedures.

By 1850, there was a thriving cloth-making industry in the New England states. In years to come, this newly formed American industry would compete with England for the markets of the world. Yet, during this period, even as the factory system grew, home handcrafting was still the prevalent means by which most goods were manufactured by Americans. Town craftsmen produced everything ranging from hats and shoes to clocks, cigars, pianos, and pottery. Operations like ironworks, flour mills, and lumberyards were small and usually family-run.

Agriculture was still the dominant means of livelihood until, roughly, between 1850 and 1865. Within this 15-year span, the mechanized factory, along with the railroad, the iron ship, and advances in electricity, brought about economic and social changes undreamed of by earlier Americans.

The Railroad Opens the Land

The widespread use of railroads and ships was the direct consequence of a metallurgical process conceived of by two men, unknown to each other and living on different continents. They were Henry Bessemer of England and William Kelly of the United States. Although others before them had investigated the possibility of converting pig iron into a less brittle, more flexible steel, Bessemer and Kelly played the crucial roles in discovering the best means to accomplish this.

The Bessemer process made it possible to manufacture steel cheaply. This meant that steel plates could be designed for larger, lighter, and faster ships. Steel beams and girders could be manufactured to build skyscrapers, and hundreds of other items could be greatly improved and made to work more effectively. Like most inventions, the process developed by Bessemer and Kelly would be further modified and improved by others.

Thanks to this new steel process and the invention of the air brake, which dramatically increased the speed at which trains could travel, railroad trains took center stage as the major means of transportation. In America, vigorously competing entrepreneurs, in financial partnerships with federal, state or city governments, created a vast network of railroad companies.

In 1850, there was very little rail travel and most train lines were in the northeast section of the country. By 1925, however, trains carrying freight and passengers were crisscrossing the country, shipping merchandise from coast to coast.

For the first time, goods that were manufactured in one part of the country could be transported, at relatively fast speeds, to many other regions. The new national markets that were formed brought about a reorganization of business practices, which now included salesmen, brokers, wholesalers, various types of middlemen, and advertisers. Before railroad travel became common, inland rivers and canals had been the major highways for commerce. The railroad connected isolated rural areas with markets and made regions of the country more accessible for settlement.

American Blacks Establish New Towns

The competition that raged between the railroad companies was often to the advantage of people who wished to buy land cheaply and settle new towns. The goal of railroad executives was to speed up the settlement of new regions of the country. This would allow them to create new markets for clients who shipped merchandise and increase the number of passengers. To achieve these aims, railroad companies that had been granted territories previously held by government agencies sold these lands at very low prices.

Like other Americans, blacks eagerly took advantage of these land bargains. Between 1877 and 1915, at least 64 towns were founded and developed by blacks. The reasons blacks were interested in establishing new settlements were similar to those that propelled white Americans to hundreds of towns throughout the 19th century. Land was readily available and much of it was inexpensive. Although some blacks viewed moving to new locations as an opportunity to avoid discrimination, most were interested in the prospect of achieving prosperity and greater independence by owning property.

PRINCIPLE 7: Entrepreneurs must be willing to take advantage of "windows of opportunity" while they are open.

Those blacks who became real-estate agents for railroad companies were eager to earn commissions on the land they sold. Their buyers, of course, were pleased to acquire good farmland on easy terms of payment. As enterprising salesmen, these black land agents sought to arouse excitement for the properties they represented. Competing with one another, they came up with increasingly more clever ways to publicize particular regions. Resourceful agents distributed thousands of handbills, regularly ran newspaper announcements, and took to the stump to deliver speeches – all to promote the special merits of their particular properties.

For example, a flier advertising land in Arkansas called on "Worthy Colored Men" to seek out the "opportunity of your life to own a rich bottom farm." The flier went on to describe in glowing terms the many benefits awaiting new settlers of the territory. Another handbill promoted land in Oklahoma by offering homes on easy terms in a place where blacks could "educate your children in order that they become noble men and women."

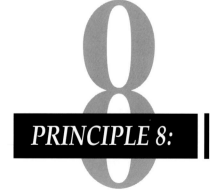

PRINCIPLE 8: | Entrepreneurs understand that successfully marketing one's product is an essential element of business.

The Montgomerys Settle Mound Bayou

Like others, blacks chose to settle new territories with their families and friends. This was true in the case of Isaiah Montgomery, who, along with his cousins, settled the town of Mound Bayou, Mississippi, in 1888. Montgomery's family was a remarkable one, and young Isaiah proved to be a natural entrepreneur.

His father and mother, Ben and Mary, were slaves on Hurricane plantation in Warren County, Mississippi, which was owned by Joe Davis. Davis was the brother of Jefferson Davis, who later became President of the Confederate States during the South's secession from 1861 to 1865.

Education is our passport to the future, for tomorrow belongs to the people who prepare for it today.

– Malcolm X

Black Settlers of Mound Bayou Had Skills Needed to Build Town

Literacy
Because Isaiah's father was literate, Isaiah learned to read and write early. As was mentioned in Chapter 3, not all slaves were savagely treated, and Isaiah enjoyed a youth similar to those of many free blacks. Even during the period of slavery, Ben Montgomery was given the freedom to build a house and a store for his family on the Davis plantation. From his trading in

merchandise, and by hiring himself out to others as a mechanic, Isaiah's father was able to pay Davis a regular sum of money, while still supporting his family.

Management Skills

Isaiah acquired his father's management skills and went to work in Joe Davis's office when he was 10 years old. While working there, he soon learned how to keep books. After Emancipation, Isaiah's father used his savings to buy a general-merchandise business in Davis Bend, Mississippi, which he named Montgomery & Sons General Store. In 1868, the Montgomery family bought Hurricane, the very plantation on which they once had lived as slaves.

Men who are in earnest are not afraid of consequences.
— Marcus Garvey

After the L.N.O. & T. Railroad Company acquired thousands of acres of land in the rich Delta region of Mississippi, the railroad's owners asked Isaiah Montgomery to act as their land agent. For his services, they were willing to pay him on a commission basis. Isaiah staked out a proposed town site and enthusiastically began selling plots of land. His first clients were people he knew who had expressed a desire to relocate.

Sales Skills

Being a good salesman, however, Isaiah did not wait for buyers to come to him. He traveled throughout Mississippi and several other states distributing fliers and handbills publicizing the town plots and surrounding farmland. Through eloquent speeches, he tried to get as many blacks as possible to see the value of working to build for themselves and their families since they were free from the restrictions of slavery. What greater value, he asked them, could there be than having the chance to own their own property? Such a proposition, he preached, would open up new opportunities for them and their children for generations to come.

Among his first land purchasers were his cousins Joshua Montgomery and Benjamin Green. Both of these men possessed skills and experience that would prove to be very helpful in the development of the new town. Joshua was born a slave in 1854. After Emancipation he apprenticed to study law and engineering. Later he practiced both of these professions. Green, who had also been a slave, lived with the Montgomery family for a while, acquired commercial skills, and became manager of Montgomery & Sons.

Creativity

All three family members decided to put their business skills and life experience to work developing the town they named Mound Bayou, after a stream that ran through the site. While they were excited and looked forward to their new entrepreneurial venture, recruiting settlers turned out to be a slow process. A plan was devised that allowed new residents to buy land from the railroad company for a specified amount per acre. Each land purchaser had five years to pay the total due. This idea, along with other creative financing techniques, enabled the new black town to be settled much faster than it normally would have been.

Opportunity follows struggle. It follows effort. It follows hard work. It doesn't come before.

— Shelby Steele

Isaiah and Green opened a sawmill business, which provided a service to the farmers who settled in the regions bordering the town, and who needed to clear their lands of trees. Thanks to the sawmill, landowners could turn their wood into building timber and many other products that they then sold for profit. In this way, many of the settlers acquired the money necessary to make the payments on their lands.

The main crop raised and sold by the farmers was cotton. As the town's population increased, more businesses were established. By 1902, eighteen businesses shipped merchandise through the Mound Bayou railroad station. The number of cotton gins grew to four and the sawmills to three. As commercial transactions increased, the need for a town bank became obvious.

Philosophy of Economic Empowerment

In 1904, Charles Banks, who believed that racial uplift was linked to economics, moved to Mound Bayou from Clarksdale, Mississippi. In Clarksdale, he had been a successful farmer. With the help of his brother, he had also operated a mercantile business. After learning about the enterprising spirit of the residents of Mound Bayou, Banks decided to relocate there. It wasn't too long before he made the necessary inroads into the banking business and teamed with some other interested parties to establish the Bank of Mound Bayou.

To create the initial funds needed to capitalize the bank, they sold shares of stock for $1 each at a meeting of the town's business leaders. This proved to be an extremely important strategic move because the bank played a key role in providing capital for new ventures and investments for the town residents. The bank also helped them survive financially bad periods such as when disease or weather prevented high yields of crops. Mound Bayou residents no longer had to go outside the town to arrange financing for businesses or homes. The bank offered reasonable credit for the purchase of farmland and town lots, and was especially helpful to those who needed small amounts of capital to get new enterprises started.

As the good reputation of the bank spread, organizations and individuals from around the State of Mississippi became depositors.

One of the bank's major depositors was the Stringer Grand Lodge. At the time, the lodge was one of the wealthiest fraternal organizations operated by blacks. The number of businesses in the town continued to grow. By 1909, there were ten general-merchandise stores, eight grocery stores, three drugstores, three shoe shops, and a bottling company. There were also tailors, seamstresses, doctors, and lawyers. In addition, there was a hotel and several lodging houses. All these businesses were owned and operated by blacks.

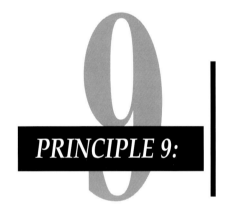

PRINCIPLE 9:

As a black entrepreneur, you must constantly look for ways to share resources with others to become self-sufficient. This was the case when the bank owners sold shares of stock to town residents.

Mound Bayou's Infrastructure

Mound Bayou was fortunate to benefit from existing communication and transportation systems, which had been established in the region. Residents had access to a public toll telephone station run by the Cumberland Telephone and Telegraph Company, and they also received mail delivery five times a week. The town's railroad depot was a very busy one, and at least six trains a day stopped there. This made the town very accessible to other regions, while facilitating the constant movement of merchandise being bought and sold by town business people. Mound Bayou became a busy commercial center.

The citizens of Mound Bayou were proud of their bank, since it not only contributed to the town's thriving business climate, but provided a model of what blacks could do for themselves. It also helped townspeople develop thrifty habits, as they learned to appreciate the connection between the accumulation of capital and the creation of wealth.

Mound Bayou is an outstanding example of the many towns founded by American blacks, towns that had their own town councils, police departments, newspapers, and banks. In every case, town leaders established rules that emphasized the necessity of working and paying one's own way. Because financial resources were limited, it was essential that every able-bodied adult pulled his and her own weight and did not become a burden to others.

Settlements like Mound Bayou were officially incorporated as towns, but others were not. Often, a group of families would decide to buy a certain amount of land in a region and a colony of sorts would spring up and eventually develop into a small community. Such communities might have under a hundred people or might grow into towns with hundreds of residents. An enterprising spirit and a readiness to work hard were the primary requirements for success, along with the ability to put off immediate wants, in order to accomplish long-term goals.

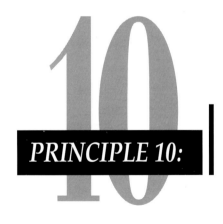

PRINCIPLE 10:

Entrepreneurs know that you must sometimes delay immediate gratification to accomplish a long-term objective of running a successful business.

Example: Rashaan wants to buy a new pair of Grant Hill sneakers, which cost $85. He has a successful lawn-mowing service, but needs to buy some additional tools to increase his productivity. He thinks he should buy the tools and wait for the sneakers, but he wants those sneakers in the worst way. What should he do?

Other Successful Black Towns

The settlers of Nicodemus, Kansas, started out in great poverty, but eventually lifted their town to economic self-sufficiency. The settlers of Dearfield, Colorado, were so poor that they first lived in tents and even in natural caves, while working at nearby farms. They were eventually able to build their own homes and establish farms.

Our elevation must be the result of self-efforts and work of our own hands. No other human power can accomplish it. If we but determine it shall be so, it will be so.
– Martin R. Delany, 1852

In contrast, Langston City, Oklahoma, was founded by blacks who were better prepared to support themselves. Within just a couple of years, they had already established a bank, several retail groceries, blacksmith shops, barbershops, restaurants, feedstores, a soap factory, two hotels and a Board of Trade. The town council also appointed a 75-man militia and a town marshal. Langston was admired for its serious, enterprising, law-abiding residents.

It took the townspeople of Hobson City, Alabama, 15 years to make their town economically solvent. They proudly boasted of their schools, churches, businesses, and waterworks, all hallmarks of what they called their "progressive town."

In Boley, Oklahoma, founded in 1904 on a proud nationalist spirit, a group of blacks, through mutual assistance, created a prosperous business community. The town's newspaper, the Boley Progress, was a major promoter of the town, urging enterprising blacks who lived in other regions to resettle in Boley. The paper's editor, O.H. Bradley, stressed the citizens' dedication to self-help and mutual cooperation. In one article, he assured prospective residents that Boley townspeople were willing to help any "industrious colored man" until "he is able to get his business in good shape."

A folk song has immortalized Boley, and catches the spirit and pride of the residents of most black towns.

Say, have you heard the story,
Of a little colored town,
Way over in the Nation
On such lovely sloping ground?

With as pretty little houses
As you ever chanced to meet,
With not a thing but colored folks
A-standing in the streets?

Oh, its a pretty country
And the Negroes own it, too,
With not a single white man here
To tell us what to do.

Towns Needed Railroad to Survive

The founding of a town was always a risky venture. More towns failed than succeeded, whether founded by blacks or whites. A town failed mainly due to unforeseen changes in social conditions or economic circumstances. Failure was almost guaranteed if the railroad shut down or moved its terminal away from the town. At this time, rail transportation was a critical key to success. Trains were the most reliable way to transport the town's produce and merchandise for sale to other regions. They were also essential for bringing into town the supplies and goods needed by the residents.

In addition, outsiders needed to have access to the town, since residents did not want to live in an area where they were cut off from relatives and friends. Of major importance to a town's economic health was the attitude of potential investors. These individuals tended to invest in properties and businesses in towns that were accessible to widespread markets. Very few towns could survive the devastating blow to its economic life that was brought on by the loss of the railroad.

The Invention Fever

The spirit of invention that gripped so many people throughout the country during the late 19th and 20th centuries was not the sole domain of one class or type of American. People from all walks of life caught the fever, including the country's black population.

American blacks shared the same concerns with others when it came to being properly acknowledged for their contributions. A common hazard faced by every inventor was the possibility of failing to get credit for one's work. This was especially true in times prior to the keeping of historical records. Very often the identity of an inventor was lost in history. In some cases, implements or tools came into common use and were modified in different ways over time. The fact that records were not always adequately prepared and kept made it difficult to determine the identity of person or persons who first conceived of the idea.

During slavery, American blacks faced an additional problem in this regard, because slaves were not permitted to patent their inventions. Therefore, we cannot know for sure just how many inventions may have been the handiwork of blacks. In spite of these restrictions, however, from the period of Emancipation onward, it is possible to trace hundreds of inventions that were registered at the United States Patent Office by innovative blacks.

Since new developments are the product of a creative mind, we must therefore stimulate and encourage that type of mind in every way possible.

— George Washington Carver

Blacks Catch the Fever Too

A talented black inventor who had an interest in engines was Granville Woods. As a young man, he, too, worked for a railroad company as a fireman and engineer. He also worked in a machine shop and attended classes in electrical and mechanical engineering at night. In 1884, Woods and his brother opened a machine shop in Cincinnati, which gave Granville the chance to concentrate his energy on experimenting with various devices. His first patent was for a steam boiler furnace that was able to operate on less fuel than that required by other furnaces.

It is critical that we take charge of our own destiny. — **David C. Wilson**

He also invented a telephone transmitter for sending messages by electricity. He was commissioned to do this work by the American Bell Telephone Company of Boston. The telephone industry considered this invention superior to other telegraphic instruments in use at that time. In addition to updating and improving earlier telegraphic equipment, Woods invented a communications device that could be used between moving trains to help reduce the danger of accidents. This invention was bought and used by railroad companies. He also created an apparatus that improved the operation of electrical streetcars.

Another of Woods's inventions, the **telegraphony**, was an instrument that combined features of the telephone and telegraph. It was purchased from him for a large sum of money by the Bell Telephone Company. This transaction helped to make him financially independent. During his lifetime, Woods was highly praised and respected for his abilities. A newspaper article claimed that his name "will be handed down to coming generations as one of the greatest inventors of his time."

Inventions and Business

This period of inventions was also an era of business, one in which true visionaries combined their genius for invention with sound business savvy. As we saw with earlier inventions, many individuals often played a part in the creation of a device before the final design was concluded. In the case of the light bulb, hundreds of inquisitive minds had tried to figure out how to pass electricity through a filament in a vacuum in order to produce a steady, dependable light. Up to this time, most indoor lighting depended upon kerosene lamps.

In 1879, Thomas Edison applied his creativity and skill to the problem. After many failed attempts, he produced a carbonized filament that was able to glow for 170 hours before it crumbled. This was the prototype for the light bulb, which was to bring light into the homes of ordinary people and lead to the world's first central electric light power station.

There is in the world no such force as the force of a man determined to rise.
— **W.E.B. DuBois**

Edison, the genius who dropped out of school after being labeled a "misfit," was an avid reader and read everything he could find about scientific subjects. When he was 12 years old, he took a job as a railroad train boy, performing general chores and running errands. After watching the railroad's telegraph machine working away with its

Morse code of dots and dashes, he learned the system and became an apprentice telegrapher.

While working at the railroad, he figured out a way to convert the dots and dashes into actual words that could be transferred to paper. After making some progress towards inventing a printer that could convert electrical signals into letters, he decided to quit his job to become a full-time inventor.

Edison, however, had more in mind than just inventing. In a time when new inventions were appearing almost daily, he understood the commercial significance of his efforts. He was a born entrepreneur and decided to seek out business people who would not only appreciate his work, but who would guide him so he might be adequately paid for his talent.

At 23, he moved from Michigan to New York City, where he became a partner in a company that agreed to manufacture his first telegraphic printer, which he called the Universal Stock Printer. This was the first of his many important inventions and came several years before he turned his attention to the light bulb.

In the coming years, Edison cooperated with others on several inventions, yet he wisely remained an independent entrepreneur throughout his busy career. Within just a few years, he perfected the first usable phonograph, dictating machine, and movie projector. His lifelong work laid the foundation for electronic inventions that would come in the 20th century.

PRINCIPLE 11:

Great ideas and inventions without basic business principles are like a kite without a tail. They simply won't fly. Edison, like all successful entrepreneurs, understood this.

By the time Edison's first printer was produced, the entire telegraph industry had become fiercely competitive as hopeful geniuses strived to be the creators of the next great invention in communications. In fact, in almost every field imaginable, Americans were enthusiastically developing ideas for appliances and mechanical gadgets. The field of electricity was an especially busy one. All kinds of electrical gadgets, motors, and machinery saw birth during this surge of creative activity.

One of these inventors was George Westinghouse, who possessed the same entrepreneurial vision as did Edison and already had an important invention to his credit, the air brake. The air brake increased the speed of trains. Less time was needed to transport goods, which resulted in more goods being delivered to eagerly awaiting consumers. With the success of the air brake, Westinghouse was able to form his own company. He then experimented with electricity. In partnership with another inventor, Nikola Tesla, Westinghouse and his company's engineers perfected the use of alternating current, which, unlike direct current, could transport electricity over long distances and at low cost. This also proved to be a very successful discovery for Westinghouse. So like most true entrepreneurs, he formed companies to produce and distribute his inventions and became a wealthy man in the process.

As the lives of many inventors make clear, business and invention go hand in hand. History reveals many striking examples of inventor-entrepreneurs. Businessman Ebenezer Butterick invented the standardized paper pattern to make clothing, which became an immediate hit with homemakers and professional dressmakers. He then established a factory to manufacture these patterns, and even started a magazine to promote their sale. Entrepreneur Willis Carrier, in 1902, formulated the basic theories of air conditioning to control temperature and humidity. In 1911, he designed a mechanical air conditioner and, in 1915, he began to manufacture it.

And, of course, the foremost entrepreneur, Henry Ford, who experimented with different car designs in a shed behind his house, has left his mark forever on the world. His Ford Motor Company could not keep up with the demand for the Model T, which he first produced in 1908. This was the first mass-produced automobile that was cheap enough to be bought by the average worker.

Ford, who established the first moving assembly line, paid his workers twice the average hourly rate, because he believed this would inspire them to greater productivity. He became a millionaire many times over and is credited with having had a major influence on the growth of manufacturing in the United States.

Everybody's Doing It

As news spread about the success of men like Edison and Westinghouse and the financial rewards they enjoyed, the age of the inventor-entrepreneur arrived. Countless stories and examples of all types of inventions were celebrated in the media. Stories were told about particular inventors' rise to riches, which was sometimes over a short period of time. The frenzy surrounding inventions created even greater numbers of people who earnestly applied themselves to developing new devices or modifying existing ones to make them more efficient.

Among the hundreds of useful inventions that the country witnessed in the latter part of the 19th century were the telephone, typewriter, calculator, refrigerator, and, of course, the automobile. During the first quarter of the 20th century alone, the United States Patent Office issued about 970,000 patents, which was more than it had issued in the past several years.

Blacks Succeed as Entrepreneurs

As we have learned, long before slavery was over, free blacks were excelling in business. For two centuries, when many slaves were freed, they observed the world around them and discovered how other Americans were achieving success through business competition. Experience soon taught them that the ownership of businesses and property would help them maintain greater control over the direction of their lives.

The tragedy in life doesn't lie in not reaching your goal. The tragedy lies in having no goal to reach. It isn't a calamity to die with dreams unfulfilled, but it is certainly a calamity not to dream. It is not a disaster to be unable to capture your ideal, but it is a disaster to have no ideal to capture.

— Benjamin E. Mays

Although their businesses were on a smaller scale than those of the whites in some cases, the ability of blacks to combine business skills with inventive thinking were critical to the success of their enterprises. William Powell, a craftsman, owned the Standard Repair Shop in Cass County, Michigan, where he repaired just about any kind of appliance or tool. In order to facilitate his work, and help him meet his customers' needs, Powell invented several mechanical implements.

Joseph Lee, in the 1880s, was the owner of three catering businesses. Bread crumbs was an item that he and his employees used constantly in various recipes. Making bread crumbs by hand was a slow, time-consuming job that could have been better spent preparing the specialties desired by their customers. Lee worked at solving the problem and finally invented his own automatic, time-saving bread-crumb maker. Like other businessmen, Powell and Lee's goal was to perform tasks faster and more efficiently so they could win more customers and increase profits.

Blacks Encounter Opposition to Business Success

For any business to grow and expand, it should have access to the largest possible consumer market. Every entrepreneur wants to reach as many potential customers as possible. Throughout the period of

46

slavery, free blacks encountered few obstacles when it came to expanding the reach of their businesses; in most cases, their primary customers were white. However, during the Reconstruction period that followed the war in the South (where most blacks lived) serious mistakes were made by politicians and other officials of the North and South. The victorious North and the conquered South shared the guilt of mishandling the resettlement of the former slaves. Some of these tragic errors in policy unfortunately led to a hardening of negative attitudes and angry reactions by both northerners and southerners towards blacks.

Many southerners accused northern politicians of imposing vengeful policies against them as punishment for the relentless battles they waged during the war. A backlash against the freed slaves ensued, resulting in the establishment of unfair, restrictive laws in some parts of the South. Although such laws had an impact on social mobility, most blacks were more concerned with restrictions that might interfere legally with their economic freedom. Laws were passed that limited their employment opportunities and their ability to conduct business. These discriminatory laws were not enforced to the same degree in every region, but they still made it harder for blacks to compete with white-owned businesses, or to expand their enterprises beyond limited borders.

Chance has never yet satisfied the hope of a suffering people. Action, self-reliance, the vision of self and the future have been the only means by which the oppressed have seen and realized the light of their own freedom.

— Marcus Garvey

In spite of these legal obstacles, a great many blacks founded businesses and succeeded as entrepreneurs. Operating within the limited boundaries that were drawn for them in certain parts of the South, they turned their segregated communities into enterprising enclaves that set the stage for future black economic development.

Black Business Before the 1965 Civil Rights Law

In Durham, North Carolina, for example, black entrepreneurs created a solid economic foundation that supported a multitude of businesses. By 1910 and into the 1950s, Durham's main black business district was a bustling and fully developed commercial center. In another part of the city, on Parish Street, there were so many black-owned stores and businesses that it was nicknamed "Negro Wall Street." All of this entrepreneurial activity was made possible because business leaders had the foresight to establish bank and loan associations. These financial companies provided support and investment opportunities for the small business owner.

PRINCIPLE 12:

Black entrepreneurs must go back to basics. The blacks who settled Mound Bayou, Mississippi, and those who created businesses in Durham created their own financial institutions. Today's black entrepreneurs must do the same.

Among Durham's most solvent businesses were the:

- **Dunbar Realty and Insurance Company**
- **Bankers Fire Insurance Company**
- **Mutual Building and Loan Association**
- **Home Modernization and Supply Company**
- **People's Building and Loan Association**
- **Southern Fidelity Mutual Insurance Company**
- **Mechanics and Farmers Bank**

The Mechanics and Farmers Bank had a tremendous influence on the business life of Durham. It provided capital for hundreds of enterprises over many years. And, during the devastating 1930s Depression, when companies were dying all across the country, Mechanics and Farmers was so well managed that it helped most of Durham's black businesses survive.

The Durham Commercial and Security Company was established to finance black-owned businesses, as was the National Negro Finance Corporation. Such institutions were formed in order to stimulate business activity within black communities throughout the country.

The largest and most successful enterprise among these very successful businesses was the North Carolina Mutual Life Insurance Company, which had been founded and managed for years by the brothers John and Ed Merrick, along with their cousins Asa and Charles Spaulding. John Merrick, who had little formal education, had been a barber until he had saved enough money to purchase a partnership in a small business, which became very prosperous. A true entrepreneur, he next purchased real-estate properties and began developing several barbering products to sell.

In 1898 he joined six other businessmen to form the North Carolina Mutual Life Insurance Company. The company opened for business in space rented for $2 a month in a medical office. When the first insurance claim for $40 came due, there was so little money in the treasury that the Merricks and other officers had to pay from their own pockets. Little did they know that by 1939 North Carolina Mutual would be a major corporation in Durham, paying over $18 million to the beneficiaries of its policyholders and employing over 1,000 people. By that time, the company had served more than a quarter million policyholders. Years of conscientious management had created a company that brought comfortable profits to its investors, while providing a much-needed service to the community.

Durham became a well-known center for black entrepreneurship, as its remarkable success was heralded around the country. The town was a

Time is neutral and does not change things. With courage and initiative, leaders change things.
– Jesse Jackson

model that others were proud to emulate. One account described Durham in this way: "Here are concentrated more business firms both in size and variety than in any other small city, and even many large cities do not have as much Negro enterprise." An enthusiastic visitor exhorted Americans to visit Durham. He wrote, "Go to Durham and see the industrious Negro at his best. Go to Durham and see the cooperative spirit among Negroes at its best."

Other Successful Black Business Centers

Between 1907 and 1921, in Tulsa, Oklahoma, black entrepreneurs created an impressive number of businesses, including:

- **Restaurants**
- **Grocery stores**
- **Hotels**
- **Theaters**
- **Real-estate firms**
- **Construction companies**
- **Printers**
- **Tailors**
- **Lawyers**
- **Dentists**
- **Medical doctors**

Other cities also saw the development of bustling black business districts. Individual entrepreneurs in cities around the country played important roles in the economic uplift of their communities. For

51

example, between 1904 and 1940 Charles Douglass provided jobs for many people through the companies he owned in Macon, Georgia. His companies included a popular theater and a hotel. Douglass believed in creating opportunity and not waiting for it to find him. He began with only a rural elementary-school education.

As a teenager, he worked as a farm laborer and a carriage driver, and in a candy factory. He managed to save enough money to buy a partnership in a small bicycle-repair shop. Applying his natural savvy and intelligence, he dabbled in real estate. Over the years he owned or leased over 100 properties.

Douglass was credited with helping Macon enlarge its business life and was well known for his special interest in business development among blacks. An associate said of him, "Mr. Douglass does not hoard his money in banks. He spends it and makes employment for our people. He has placed his money in circulation in business where it can bless the people."

S.B. Fuller, who started his door-to-door cosmetics business with $25 during the 1930s Depression, became so successful that eventually he employed thousands of blacks. A born salesman, he willingly taught others the art of selling. His Fuller Products Company did business in almost every state, and he became a wealthy man. Like many other blacks who were dedicated to self-help, Fuller was a firm believer in the power of business to transform communities. He also helped many new entrepreneurs to establish their own small businesses. Fuller believed that one could be a greater asset to society by becoming prosperous than by remaining poor.

As a slave, Elizabeth Keckley had been a superlative dressmaker. After Emancipation, she opened a business in Washington, D.C., where she designed clothing for some of the most prominent residents of the city. Her services were much sought after, and over the years, her successful business provided employment for many tailors and seamstresses.

In Virginia, in 1902, John Mitchell founded the Mechanics Savings Bank, through which he counseled blacks on how to wisely invest their money. He supervised the investments of self-help fraternal groups. It was his goal to keep such groups solvent so they could continue in the economic role they played in the community.

Another banker who thought it his duty to encourage thrift and the wise use of money was William Pettiford. After becoming head of the Alabama Penny Loan and Savings Bank in 1899, Pettiford set out to educate his depositors in finance, while providing them loans for home building and business development. He said it was his goal to "stimulate a wholesome desire among our people to become property owners and substantial citizens."

One of America's most famous entrepreneurs was Sarah Breedlove Walker, popularly known as Madame C.J. Walker. After experimenting with various formulas to straighten hair, in 1905 she created one that worked. She set about selling it door-to-door, eventually hiring others to help her. In this way, she helped many people start their own cosmetics and hair-care businesses. In 1910, in Indianapolis, Indiana, Madame

I had to make my own living and my own opportunity . . . Don't sit down and wait for the opportunities to come; you have to get up and make them.

– Madame C.J. Walker

Walker built a plant to manufacture her hair-care products. Eventually Walker industries employed over 3,000 people and she became a millionaire.

Madame Walker was well known for her philanthropy and built homes for the aged in St. Louis and Indianapolis. She also established a YMCA in Indianapolis, maintained scholarships for needy students, and gave cash awards to any of her employees who performed community service.

Charles Smiley, a Chicago businessman, owned the most popular catering business in the city. To learn the business, he hired himself out during the day as a waiter at catered dinners, while working at night as a janitor. As a result, he established his own contacts and gradually built a very successful business, which provided employment to hundreds of workers. Eventually, he owned a fleet of 16 horses for his delivery wagons. In many cities, the catering trade was monopolized by blacks who earned fortunes by their skillful management of banquets, weddings, and other special occasions.

In New York City, Philip Payton played an important economic role as a Realtor who owned several Harlem apartment buildings. In the 1920s, he and a group of other black Realtors prevented the eviction of dozens of black tenants by bigoted landlords by purchasing the buildings in which the tenants lived. Payton was hailed for intelligently using economic clout to defeat racism.

Another Realtor who practiced self-help was John Whitelaw Lewis. In Washington, D.C., discrimination laws prevented blacks from using hotels in the city. Lewis, a black businessman, decided to remedy the situation by building a first-rate hotel, which was designed by a black architect and constructed by black tradesmen. For many years, the Whitelaw Hotel, which opened in 1919, was the center of fashionable life for professional blacks in Washington. By taking the initiative, Lewis turned the tables on bigotry, showing blacks how to use money and ingenuity to subvert racism.

After graduating from high school and teaching for a few years, Maggie Lena Walker found herself drawn to the world of business. In 1899, she became an officer of the Independent Order of St. Luke, a fraternal business organization. In 1902, she was made president of the St. Luke Penny Savings Bank in Richmond, Virginia. Under her management, the bank prospered and played an important financial role in the Richmond community. While president of the bank, she was elected head of the Order of St. Luke. She transformed this small group with about 3,000 paid members into an influential organization with over 100,000 members. Not only did the St. Luke Order provide funds to assist in the health care and funerals of its members, it also served as a "thrift club" for members' savings. By 1924, about 15,000 children were enrolled in the club. The organization also employed 55 clerks in its home office and 145 field workers.

Among ethnic groups in America, fraternal organizations were common. Blacks discovered that the best way to help one another was to form cooperative associations of various kinds. From as early as the 18th century, blacks also formed mutual-aid societies similar to the St. Luke Order of Richmond. By joining such groups, they were able to provide financial lending services and assistance to one another in time of need.

One of the first of these societies founded by blacks was in Philadelphia in the 18th century. By 1838, there were 100 such groups in that city.

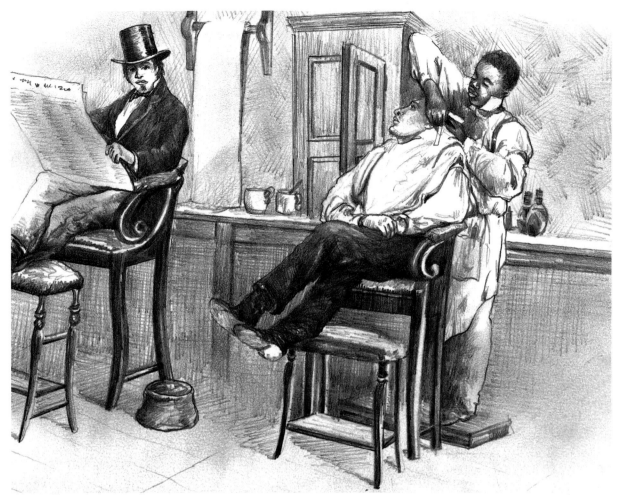

The primary goal of some groups was to provide funds for members to buy or build homes and to cope with emergencies, while others were specifically directed toward providing funds for business development. This concern for economic progress stemmed from a tradition already in place before Emancipation. During the slavery period, free blacks had been encouraged by the leading people of their communities to go into business. Martin Delaney, a leader in the 1850s, informed his fellow blacks, "If a knowledge of all the various business enterprises, trades, professions, and sciences is necessary for the elevation of the white, a knowledge of them is also necessary for the elevation of the colored man; and he cannot be elevated without them."

After slavery, this call to cooperative action was taken up by the prominent educator Booker T. Washington. Throughout the early years of this century, Washington urged blacks to create a special niche for themselves in the American economy. As director of the Tuskegee Institute, the outstanding educational center in Alabama, he became the major promoter of education and business enterprise. Because financial resources were scarce among blacks, Washington stressed the critical importance of group solidarity. He noted that, among other ethnic groups, mutual cooperation was the key to success in all endeavors. So he figured that blacks could benefit from this philosophy as well.

Washington encouraged blacks to start building with the skills and talents they already possessed. It was well known that during slavery blacks had been trained as craftsmen in just about every field. They were the carpenters, blacksmiths, shoemakers, barbers, tailors, stonemasons, and builders upon whom others depended. A study of this period concluded that "As a result of about two-and-a-half centuries of slavery, up to the outbreak of the Civil War, the knowledge of these skills was concentrated almost exclusively in the hands of the Negroes, free and slave." It was these people whom Washington was determined to help direct into productive occupations. Tuskegee students were trained in technical skills, and its graduates went on to spread Tuskegee's philosophy of economic uplift in schools around the country.

No race that has anything to contribute to the markets of the world is long in any degree ostracized. It is important and right that all privileges of the law be ours, but it is vastly more important that we be prepared for the exercises of these privileges. The opportunity to earn a dollar in a factory just now is worth infinitely more than the opportunity to spend a dollar in an opera house.

— Booker T. Washington

Washington and other black leaders of the day taught that self-help was the key to future success. They urged every black to commit himself to the discipline of work, no matter how modest or menial the labor. As we have seen, vast numbers of blacks did exactly this, as they founded and maintained small crafts and service businesses throughout the country. Many of the business people mentioned in the preceding chapters were strongly influenced by the Tuskegee philosophy of self-help.

By 1900, there were so many blacks in business that the Tuskegee leaders formed the National Negro Business League. Its purpose was to help men and women get started in their own enterprises, and to assist those already in business to become more effective entrepreneurs.

Tuskegee's Special Mission

Black farmers were another group in need of guidance. Washington and the Tuskegee leaders focused on their problems as well. Farmers, as sellers of the crops they grew, were also business people. Washington taught that economic independence should be the goal of every farmer. At the time, most blacks were tenant farmers and did not own the land on which they worked. In many cases, these farmers would grow just enough crops to pay their rent to the landowner. Washington encouraged them to raise more crops to sell for a profit, so they could save money to buy their own properties. He would tell them, "Take a load of produce to town to exchange for those items that you cannot raise. Start a bank account and put aside a little money each year until you get enough to buy a piece of land, even if it is but one acre."

The Movable School

Tuskegee established an extension service in order to bring education to poor farmers in the rural outback. The "Movable School" was a wagon that was equipped with the necessary tools and implements to teach poor farmers how to use the latest methods and equipment to expand the amount of crops they grew. Farm families were also assisted in renovating their dilapidated cabins. Thanks to the knowledge and information brought to them by the Movable School team, many farmers improved their economic circumstances and raised their standard of living.

Tuskegee was more than just an educational institution. It was the spearhead of a movement that inspired blacks around the country to work for the "progress of the race." Wherever blacks needed assistance, they knew they could turn to the multi-talented staff at Tuskegee for advice and guidance. Those who supported the goals of Tuskegee believed in a saying made famous by Washington, that is often considered the motto of the Tuskegee movement: "We must not allow our grievances to overshadow our opportunities."

Knowledge is the key that unlocks all the doors. It doesn't matter what you look like or where you come from if you have knowledge.

– Benjamin Carson

Important Dates in Black Business History

1651 Ex-slave Anthony Johnson is believed to be the first African American entrepreneur. According to various historical accounts, he accumulated enough capital to buy 250 acres of land on the Pungoteague River in Northhampton County, Virginia.

1736 Emmanuel and Mary Bernoon opened the first Oyster and Ale House in Providence, Rhode Island.

1783 Born a slave in New Orleans, James Derham became the first African American to open a medical practice.

1787 The Free African Society of Philadelphia was formed as the first mutual-aid society to support economic-development activity for the African American community.

1810 The first African-owned insurance company, called The Afro-American Insurance Company, was started in Philadelphia by James Porter, William Coleman, and Joseph Randolph.

1821 Thomas Jenning of New York City was the first African American to be issued a patent. His invention improved the dry-cleaning process for clothes.

1838 David Ruggles published the first African American newspaper in New York city, called the Mirror of Liberty.

1841 William A. Liedesdorff, the first African American millionaire, arrived in California from the Virgin Islands that year. In addition to his starting several business ventures – running a steamboat; owning a racehorse; and opening the first hotel in the city – he was a member of the city council and helped to open the first school.

1867 Two of America's most successful female entrepreneurs was born the same year. Madame C.J. Walker became the first African American female entrepreneur by managing a very successful enterprise that manufactured hair products for African American women.

Another Walker, Maggie Lena, was the first African American female to head a bank. The Richmond, Virginia, native became the president of the St. Luke's Penny Savings Bank in 1903.

1888 The first African American bank was organized in Washington, D.C.

1900 Booker T. Washington started the National Negro Business League to encourage and support the establishment of black business.

1933 H. Naglor Fitzhugh was the first African American to earn a master's degree from Harvard Business School. He worked as a vice president of marketing at Pepsi-Cola for several years.

1969 Parks Sausage became the first African American company to be publicly owned and traded on the stock market.

1970 Joseph L. Searles, III, an aide to former New York mayor John Lindsay, became the first African American to be granted a seat on the New York Stock Exchange.

1971 Johnson Products, a Chicago-based company that makes personal grooming products and cosmetics, became the first African American business to be listed on the American Stock Exchange.

1972 Jerome Holland, Ph.D., former president of Hampton University and Delaware State University, became the first African American to become a director of the New York Stock Exchange.

1991 The Black Entertainment Network (BET), owned by Robert Johnson, became the first African American company to be listed on the New York Stock Exchange.

1992 Entrepreneur Reginald Lewis, the founder and CEO of TLC Beatrice International, became the first African American businessman to be listed in Forbes Magazine's list of the nation's 400 wealthiest people. At the time he had personal assets of $400 million.

Contemporary Black Entrepreneurs

So few of us can understand what it takes to make a man . . . the man who will never say die; the man who will never give up; the man who will never depend upon others to do for him what he ought to do for himself; the man who will not blame God, who will not blame Nature, will not blame Fate for his condition; but the man who will go out and make conditions to suit himself.

— Marcus Garvey

General Manufacturing/Distribution

Loida Nicolas Lewis
Chairperson/CEO,
TLC Beatrice International Holdings, Inc.
- International food processor and distributor
- Founded 1987
- $2.1 billion in revenue
- 4,500 employees
- Located in New York, New York

David Bing
CEO and Chairman, the Bing Group
- Manufacturer of steel structures for automobile exteriors
- Founded 1980
- $101,000 million in revenue
- 450 employees
- Located in Detroit, Michigan

The next time you get into a new car, think about David Bing. Chances are, his company had a hand in making some of the steel exterior parts of the car.

As the owner of an already successful manufacturing company, David Bing believed that his company could be stronger and more competitive by merging with Regal Plastics Company out of Detroit, Michigan, another black-owned business specializing in manufacturing plastic interior automobile parts. So whether you're looking at the outside or inside of a new car, the new company, Bing Manufacturing, probably built some of the parts.

Earl Graves
Part Owner, Pepsi-Cola
- Soft-drink distributor
- Started in 1990 with partnering agreement with Magic Johnson
- 160 employees
- $51 million in sales

In addition to his Black Enterprise Magazine empire, Earl Graves expanded his entrepreneurial wings in the soft-drink distribution business. He teamed up with several top-notch black businessmen, including Magic Johnson, a former Los Angeles Lakers NBA superstar, to start the business. Graves proves that once you catch entrepreneurial fever, chances are you will own at least one or several businesses.

Leon Tupper
President/CEO and Majority Owner,
Gilreath Manufacturing
- Acquired in 1991
- Supplies plastic parts to automotive industry
- $17 million in sales
- 157 employees

Tupper always dreamed of owning a company. As manager of sales and marketing at Gilreath Manufacturing, he got a chance to run the company when the Board of Directors fired the executive officers and appointed him CEO. He turned the company around, bringing it out of bankruptcy, and is now majority owner. "Opportunity comes in strange shapes and sizes," he says. "You have to be vigilant to recognize it."

Finance

Ernesta Procope
President, E.G. Bowman Insurance Brokerage Firm
- Largest black-owned insurance brokerage company
- Founded 1953
- 44 employees
- $36 million in sales
- Located in New York, New York

Fighting against the odds, Ernesta Procope was the first black woman in the country to head her own insurance brokerage firm when she started the company in 1953. Like most entrepreneurs, Ernesta is no stranger to trouble and hard times. She almost lost her business in the 1960s during the riots when many of the insurers started canceling their accounts. With strong determination, she appealed to the governor to initiate insurance reform, which stabilized the insurance industry and helped save her business. Today her company is successful and going strong.

Emma C. Chappell
Founder and CEO,
United Bank of Philadelphia
- Started in 1992
- 76 employees
- $92 million in assets

Entertainment and Publishing

Russell Simmons
CEO, Rush Communications
- Rap and hip-hop entertainment
- Founded 1982
- Second largest black-owned entertainment company
- $34 million in revenue
- 70 employees
- Located in New York, New York

Not settling for the success and rewards of his entertainment company, Russell Simmons started another company, Rush Media, an advertising agency focusing on the urban marketplace. He will undoubtedly use his entrepreneurial savvy to make his advertising agency as successful as his hip-hop entertainment company. Russell is living proof that you can make money and love what you do at the same time.

Earl G. Graves
Editor and Publisher, Earl G. Graves Ltd.
- Magazine-publishing company
- Founded 1970
- $29 million in sales
- 70 employees
- Located in New York, New York

As owner and publisher of Black Enterprise Magazine, Earl G. Graves is credited with having the first successful magazine focusing on black entrepreneurs. Offering tips, ideas, resources, and information vital to black entrepreneurship, Black Enterprise Magazine is sometimes referred to as the Black Bible of Black Business.

Retailing

Karl Kani
Owner and Designer, Karl Kani Infinity
- Fashion-design company
- Founded 1993
- $59 million in sales
- 19 employees

Karl Kani's customers, like him, are street smart and love stylish fashions. Kani is credited with helping the company, Cross Colours, rise to national prominence. After that company experienced difficulty due to poor financial planning, Kani struck out on his own and formed Karl Kani Infinity. Since his days at Cross Colours, he has not missed a beat and has an impressive list of devoted customers who add to his success each day.

Franchising

Warren Thompson
President, Thompson Hospitality, L.P.
- Largest minority-owned franchised food operation in the United States
- 27 Shoney franchises
- 2,000 employees
- $40 million in annual sales

Thompson knew at the age of 10 that he wanted to be in business, the restaurant business in particular. As a former executive for the Marriott Corporation, he found that he was not satisfied with being just another employee. Thompson thought he might own a couple of franchises at first. However, as his ambition grew, so did his entrepreneurial zeal. Using his skills and desire to be in business for himself, he successfully negotiated deals with Marriott to buy more and more restaurants. And today, at 36, Thompson is owner of Thompson Hospitality, which operates 27 Shoney franchises, serving 20,000 customers a day.

Car Dealerships

Alvin S. Smith
CEO, Al Smith Chevrolet-Oldsmobile, Inc.
- Ranked number 1 in 1996 as the biggest black-owned automobile dealer
- Started in 1986
- 28 employees
- $408 million in sales
- Located in Brighton, Colorado

Jesse A. Moore
CEO, Warner Robins Oldsmobile-Cadillac-
Pontiac-GMC Truck, Inc.
- Ranked number 2 on Black Enterprise list of top-20 black-owned auto dealers
- Started in 1991
- 50 employees
- $400 million in sales
- Located in Warner Robins, Georgia

Mel Farr Sr.
CEO, Mel Farr Automotive GroupMC Truck, Inc.
- Ranked number 3 on Black Enterprise list of top-20 black-owned auto dealers
- Started in 1975
- 495 employees
- $382 million in sales
- Located in Oak Park, Michigan

Alvin Smith, Jesse Moore, and Mel Farr all realized that blacks make up a significant part of the customer base for the automobile industry. They saw no reason that blacks should always be consumers of automobiles instead of owning automobile dealerships. With an uncompromising desire to be in business for themselves, they set out to own and operate dealerships. Each of them has a unique story, and all three have risen to the top of the industry, representing the top-3 black-owned auto dealers in the country for 1996.

Sports

Magic Johnson
NBA Franchise Owner, Los Angeles Lakers
- Acquired 5% ownership in 1994 for $10 million
- Owner of Magic Johnson T's and official T-shirt licensee of the NBA and NFL
- Part owner of Pepsi-Cola of Washington, D.C., in partnership with Earl G. Graves
- $51 million in sales
- 160 employees

Al Toon
Former wide receiver for the New York Jets
- Owner of four Burger King franchises
- One of eight investors to open a new, independently owned bank in Madison, Wisconsin
- Owner of a thriving real-estate business for the last 10 years
- Part owner of NBA Denver Nuggets basketball team

Isaiah Thomas
Former player with the Detroit Pistons NBA team
- 10% owner of Toronto Raptors NBA team
- Ownership asset equals $12.5 million
- Also vice–president and general manager of team

What all three of these former sports superstars have in common is that although they knew being a player was fine, being an owner was better. As players, they earned a living by working for someone else. As owners, they still earn an excellent living but now others work for them. Unlike being a player-employee on a team, their ownership status gives them freedom, flexibility, and financial independence.

Tribute to Two Fallen Champions of Entrepreneurship

It has been said that the mark of a great leader is his or her legacy after departing this life. That certainly is true of two of the most notable African leaders, Ronald H. Brown and Reginald Lewis.

Ronald H. Brown

"Ron Brown . . . was continually reaching out trying to bridge the differences between people, always trying to get the best out of people, always believing that we could do more than we have done . . . Ron Brown . . . [used] the power of the Commerce Department to find ways to give opportunity to ordinary Americans, to generate jobs for the American economy and build better futures for American citizens . . . He was one of the best advisors and ablest people I ever knew . . . And he always believed that his mission in life was to put people's dreams within their reach if they were willing to work for it and believe in themselves."

— President Clinton, April 3, 1996

Brown will be remembered as the first African American to serve as head of the U.S. Department of Commerce. A lawyer and skillful negotiator, Brown led several trade missions to foreign countries and paved the way for long-term economic growth by building strong trading partnerships with those foreign trading partners. Brown will also be remembered as a strong advocate of small business and minority small business in particular. He firmly believed that the answer to many of the problems in the urban cities is a strong economic base that provides long-term employment opportunities for everyone. But he went beyond that, to forge public-private partnerships, helping create millions of American jobs. Since January, 1993, Ron Brown had worked tirelessly, shoulder-to-shoulder with American business, to eliminate barriers and open new markets for American businesses around the world.

Reginald Lewis

Like Ron Brown, Reginald Lewis understood that one answer to the problems African Americans face in America is economic empowerment. At an early age, Lewis had known that he would be in business. As a Harvard University graduate with an MBA, Lewis used his business skills to start an investment banking company on Wall Street. He had a reputation for putting together huge investment deals that were normally done by much larger Wall Street firms. Lewis approached each deal with a keen eye for detail. His employees knew he would catch any mistakes they made so they worked hard to please him. It wasn't long before Lewis had turned a small investment management company into a multimillion-dollar firm with an impressive list of Wall Street clients. By the time of his death in 1993, TLC Beatrice International was a multibillion-dollar enterprise with offices in Europe as well as the United States. Shortly before his death, Lewis had co-authored a book entitled "Why Should White Guys Have All the Fun?" This book speaks of the type of individual Lewis was. He knew that one's color might be an impediment to economic progress, but he believed it should never be an excuse for failure. Lewis made it clear that he wanted to be judged by his abilities and intellect and not the color of his skin. Many African Americans say that they are just as good as whites, but Lewis believed it.

Top Ten Black Firms in 1996

∎

1   **TLC BEATRICE INTERNATIONAL HOLDINGS, INC.**
New York–based: international food processor and distributor
1995 earnings: $2.2 billion
Loida Lewis, Chief Executive Officer

2   **JOHNSON PUBLISHING COMPANY, INC.**
Chicago, Illinois–based: publishing, broadcasting, TV production, cosmetics and hair-care firm
1995 earnings: $326 million
John H. Johnson, Publisher and Chief Executive Officer

3   **PHILADELPHIA COCA-COLA BOTTLING CO. INC.**
Philadelphia, Pennsylvania–based: soft-drink bottler
1995 earnings: $325 million
Bruce Llewellyn, Chief Executive Officer

4   **Pulsar Data Systems, Inc.**
Lanham, Maryland–based: computer systems integration and network design firm
1995 earnings: $166 million

5   **H. J. RUSSELL AND COMPANY**
Atlanta, Georgia–based: construction, property management, airport concessions, and real-estate development firm
1995 earnings: $164 million
Herman J. Russell, Chief Executive Officer

6   **UNIWORLD GROUP**
New York–based: advertising, promotion, event marketing and direct-response firm
1995 earnings: $158 million

7   **GRANITE BROADCASTING CORP.**
New York–based: network television affiliates firm
1995 earnings: $155 million

8   **CONVENIENCE CORPORATION OF AMERICA**
West Palm Beach, Florida–based: convenience stores
1995 earnings: $137 million

9   **BURRELL COMMUNICATIONS GROUP INC.**
Chicago, Illinois–based: advertising, public-relations and marketing firm
1995 earnings: $135 million

10 **BET HOLDINGS, INC.**
Washington, D.C.–based: cable television, network and magazine-publishing firm
1995 earnings: $133 million
Robert Johnson, Chief Executive Officer

Source: Black Enterprise Magazine, 1997

What's Next

In the preceding chapters you have been introduced to black entrepreneurship and discovered the rich history of African Americans in business. You have read about the success stories of individuals who had tremendous odds against them, including slavery and being denied the right to patent their inventions. In spite of these obstacles, African Americans managed to own businesses and provided opportunities for future generations. This legacy should not be forgotten. Black men and women today must take advantage of the many opportunities to start their own businesses. As society becomes more dependent on technology and as corporations continue to downsize, one of the most reliable ways left to make a living is to create a business for oneself. What about you? Are you ready to become an entrepreneur? If so, let us show you the next step.

Suggested Activities to Help Expose Black Youth to Entrepreneurship

This section will give you suggestions about how adults can help you to become better prepared for the world of entrepreneurship. Learning how to start and manage a small enterprise will require the support and encouragement of others in your community. Successful entrepreneurs know how to respond when asked, "How can I help you with your business?" You must be prepared to answer this question. Here are some examples of how adults and community organizations can help you to become a successful entrepreneur. Make sure that you share these ideas with your parents, neighbors, relatives, teachers, and other interested adults.

For Parents:

✔ Expose your child to entrepreneurial magazines like Black Enterprise. Discuss the contents of the magazine and other business-related topics on a regular basis. Make theses discussion a part of the dinner conversation.

✔ With your child, visit black-owned businesses in your community and in other cities when you are on vacation or visiting relatives.

✔ Create contractual/entrepreneurial opportunities for your children at home. Use this method of teaching them about work and business instead of giving them a weekly allowance.

✔ Start a part-time business with your child. Some examples of successful parent/child business partnerships have been in retailing clothes, delivering newspapers, making silk flower arrangements, janitorial services, etc.

✔ If you are unable to share a business experience with your child, find a business mentor within your family or network of friends. Check with black business/professional organizations like the local Black CAP Association, Black MBA Association and Black Chamber of Commerce.

✔ Ask teachers to identify entrepreneurial curriculum materials to teach with core subjects. Encourage the school to start entrepreneur clubs and after-school programs.

✔ Work with churches and/or other spiritual institutions in your community to establish a Youth Enterprise Center. Churches have all the necessary ingredients to serve as a youth business incubator: customers, equipment, space, mentors, etc.

For Teachers:

✔ Request your principal to start an entrepreneur course.

✔ Develop ways to incorporate entrepreneurial principles within core subjects.

✔ Identify and invite black entrepreneurs in the community to speak to students.

For Black Churches:

✔ Create a Youth Enterprise Center with the church structure.

✔ Have church members adopt and support youth businesses.

For Black Politicians:

✔ Write and promote legislation for mandatory entrepreneurship training.

For Black Social and Fraternal Organizations:

✔ Find an entrepreneurial program in your community and volunteer as a business mentor.

✔ Support entrepreneurship exposure and training programs at your local schools or start a program at your church or community center.

✔ Make work opportunities available to neighborhood youth enterprises. Some examples of contracts with youth are house painting, babysitting, office window cleaning, and computer work (graphics design and word processing).

✔ Be a good example and role model. Start a part-time business of your own.

Business Ideas for Youth Entrepreneurs

Babysitting	Disc Jockey	Office Organizers
Babyproofing Services	Dog Walking	Personal Shopping
Button Making	Errand Services	Photography
Cake Decorators	Furniture Painting	Selling Novelties
Calligraphy Services	Graffiti Removal	Silk Flower Arrangements
Candy Shop	Handbill Delivery	Silkscreening
Car Detailing	Homework Helper	Singing Telegrams
Catering	House Painting	Snow Removal
Cleaning Services	Jewelry Making	Telemarketing
Clothing Alterations	Kitchen Cleaners	Translation Services
Computers	Landscaping	Videotaping Services
Companion Services	Lawn Care	Wallpapering
Cookie Making	Mailing Services	Window Washing
Copying Services	Making Crafts	Word Processing
Curb Painting	Making Gift Baskets	
Desktop Publishing	Monogramming	

For more ideas read Module Three of <u>The New Youth Entrepreneur Curriculum</u> called "Business Ideas for All Communities," developed by EDTEC, Inc., and the Center for Entrepreneurial Leadership, Ewing Kauffman Foundation. This module helps the young entrepreneur:

✔ Explore multiple entrepreneurial activities for young people.

✔ Define aspects of entrepreneurial ventures and explain why each is important.

✔ Select and analyze an entrepreneurial opportunity according to the aspects studied.

✔ Identify at least one entrepreneurial idea which fits the individual's neighborhood, interest, abilities, and goals.

Some Good Things to Read

Black Enterprise Magazine. Available at newsstands or from 130 Fifth Avenue, New York, New York 10011-4399;1-800-727-7777.

Why Should White Guys Have All the Fun? Story of Reginald Lewis's life from his East Baltimore youth through Harvard University and eventually as the owner of a multinational, multibillion-dollar business. Published by John Wiley & Sons; available in bookstores.

African American Firsts. Unsung triumphs of famous and little-known black Americans. Written by Joan Potter with Constance Claytor, published by Pinto Press, Elizabethtown, New York; available in bookstores.

The New Youth Entrepreneur. A soup-to-nuts series of workbooks for youth on how to start a business. Published by the Center for Entrepreneurial Leadership at the Ewing Marion Kauffman Foundation and the Education, Training and Enterprise Center (EDTEC). Contact EDTEC, 313 Market Street, Camden, New Jersey 08102; 1-800-963-9361.

Think and Grow Rich: A Black Choice. Written by Dennis Kimbro and Napoleon Hill. Published by Ballantine Books, New York, 1991.

Additional Resources

Internet Sites That Support Black Youth Entrepreneurship

General Search Engines

http://home,netscape.com/home/internet-search.html
    Net Search

http://altavista.digital.com
    AltaVista Search: Main Page

http://www.infoseek.com
    Infoseek

http://www.lycos.com
    Welcome to Lycos

http://index.opentext.net/allinone
    The Open Text Index

http://www.albany.net/allinone
    All-in One Search Page

http://www.hotbot.com
    HotBot - Results

Entrepreneurship Resources

http://www.csupomona.edu/ace
> Association of Collegiate Entrepreneurs

http://www.celcee.edu/index.html
> CELCEE - ERIC Clearinghouse

http://aristotle.es.twsu.edu/home/student/entre/main.html
> Center for Entrepreneurship - Wichita, KS

http://loki.stuart.iitedu/coleman/#BMARK7
> Coleman Foundation - List of Contacts

http://www.edtecinc.com
> Education, Training and Enterprise Center, Inc.

http://www.gse.ucla.edu/ERIC/contact,.html
> ERIC Clearinghouse - Community Colleges

http://www.slu.edu/eweb/big6.htm
> EWEB:Entrepreneurship's Big 6 WWW

http://www.emkf.org
> Ewing Marion Kauffman Foundation

http:/www.inc.com:80
> Inc. Online: Web - Growing Companies

http://coe.ohio-state.edu/cete/entre/index.htm
> Ohio State University Entrepreneurship Education

http://pages.prodigy.com/start-up
> Start Up Education

http:// pages.prodigy.com/start-up/teacher.htm
> Teacher Links

http:// www.yeo.org/resources/entreso.htm
> Young Entrepreneurs Organization

http://www.winternet.com:80/~jannmart/network.html
> Young Entrepreneurs Program Network

Internet Sites to Support Black Youth Entrepreneurship

http://www.aawc.com
> African American Haven (where to find all of the African American business links)

http://www.blackenterprise.com
> Black Enterprise Magazine (major African American magazine)

http://www.sealink,org/sea/geniinfo.htm
> California Entrepreneurship Academy

http://www.Tonybrown.com
> Tony Brown's Journal

http://www2.ari.net/cirm
> Creative Investment Research (listing of black-owned banks)

http://www.edtecinc.com
> Education, Training and Enterprise Center, Inc.

http://www.emkf.org
> Ewing Marion Kauffman Foundation

http://www.famu.edu.ced/famudrs.htm
> Florida A and M University – Youth Program

http://www.bschool.howard.edu/bus_info
> Hill's African American Sites (Howard University African American links)

Small Business Administration (SBA) Internet Resources

http://www.sbaonline.sba.gov
> Small Business Administration Home Page, source of small business data

http://www.sbaonline.sba.gov/ADVO/news
> SBA Advocacy Newsletter

http://www.sbaonline.sba.gov/ADVO/stats
> SBA Statistics on Small Business

http://www.sbaonline.sba.gov/hotlist/busstart.html
> SBA Business Startup Hotlist

http://www.sbaonline.sba.gov/ADVO/stats/fact1.html

National Black Business-Related Organizations in Support of Entrepreneurship

1) **Association of African-American
   Women Owned Business Owners**
   Post Office Box 13933
   Silver Spring, MD 20911-3933
   (301) 565-0258

2) **Association of Black CPA Firms**
   Suite 700
   1101 Connecticut Avenue
   Washington, DC 20036
   (202) 857-1100

3) **International Association of Black Business Educators**
   3810 Palmira Lane
   Silver Spring, MD 20906

4) **Interracial Opportunity for Business Opportunity**
   Suite 2212
   51 Madison Avenue
   New York, NY 10010
   (800) 252-4226
   Fax (212) 779-4365

5) **National Association of Free Enterprise**
   1322 Vermont Avenue NW
   Washington, DC 20005
   (202) 483-5700

6) **National Association of Black Accountants**
   Suite 150
   220 I Street NE
   Washington, DC 20002
   (202) 546-6222
   Fax (202) 547-1041

7) **National Association of Black Owned Broadcasters**
   Room 412
   1730 M Street NW
   Washington, DC 20036
   (202) 463-8970

8) **National Association of Black Women Entrepreneurs**
    Post Office Box 1375
    Detroit, MI 48231
    (313) 341-7400
    Fax (313) 342-3433

9) **National Association of Investment Companies**
    Suite 700
    1111 14th Street NW
    Washington, DC 20005
    (202) 289-4336

10) **National Association of Market Developers**
    Suite 500
    1422 West Peachtree Street NW
    Atlanta, GA 30309
    (404) 892-0244
    Fax (404) 874-7100

11) **National Association of Minority Contractors**
    Suite 200
    1333 F Street NW
    Washington, DC 20004
    (202) 347-8259
    Fax (202) 628-1876

12) **National Association of Minority Women in Business**
    Suite 200
    906 Grand Avenue
    Kansas City, Missouri 64106
    (816) 421-3335
    Fax (816) 421-3336

13) **National Association of Negro Business and
    Professional Women's Club**
    1806 New Hampshire Avenue NW
    Washington, DC 20009
    (202) 483-4206
    Fax (202) 462-7253

14) **National Bankers Association**
    1802 T Street NW
    Washington, DC 20009
    (202) 588-5432
    Fax (202) 588-5443

15) **National Black Chamber of Commerce**
   5741 Telegraph Avenue
   Oakland, CA 94609-1709
   Fax (510) 444-5741

16) **National Business League**
   Suite 605
   1629 K Street
   Washington, DC 20006
   (202) 466-5487

17) **National Minority Business Council**
   235 East 42nd Street
   New York, NY 10017
   (212) 573-2385
   Fax (212) 573-4462

Addtional Resource Material

Periodicals

Dollars and Sense Magazine
1610 E. 79th Street
Chicago, Illinois 60649
Ph   (312) 375-6800
Fax (312) 375-7149

Minorities and Women in Business

Venture X, Inc.
P.O. Drawer 210
Burlington, North Carolina 27216
Ph (919) 229-1462
Fax (919) 222-7455

Minority Business Entrepreneur
924 North Market Street
Inglewood, California 90302
Ph   (310) 673-9398
Fax (310) 673-0170

Newsletters

Making Success Happen Newsletter
National Association of Black Women Entrepreneurs
P.O. Box 1375
Detroit, Michigan 48231
Ph (313) 341-7400
Fax (313) 342-3433

Minorities in Business Insider
CD Publications
8204 Fenton Street
Silver Spring, Maryland 20910
Ph (301) 588-6380
(800) 666-6380
Fax (301) 588-6385

Profits
Small Business Development
Howard University
PO Box 748
Washington, DC 20059
Ph (202) 806-1653
Fax (202) 806-1777

Today
National Association of Minority Women In Business
906 Grande Avenue - Suite 200
Kansas City, Missouri 64106
Ph (816) 421-3335

Directories

African American Blackboard International Reference Guide
National Publication Sales Agency, Inc.
1610 East 79th Street
Chicago, Illinois 60649
Ph (312) 375-6800
Fax (312) 375-7149

American League of Financial Institutions
Directory of Members and Associate Members
U.S. League of Financial Institutions
1709 New York Ave. SW, Suite 801
Washington, DC
Ph (202) 628-5624

Black Enterprise -Top Black Business Issue
Earl Graves Publishing Company
130 5th Avenue, 10th Floor
New York, New York 10011
Ph (212) 242-8000
Fax (212) 989-8410

Buyers Guide to Minority Businesses
Arizona Minority Supplier Development Council
5151 North 16th Street, Suite 124
Phoenix, Arizona 85016
Ph (602) 277-8599

Caribbean Business Directory and Yellow Pages
Caribbean Publishing Company
9500 South Dadeland Blvd., Suite 500
Miami, Florida 33156
Ph (305) 670-4889

Caribbean Exporters, Importers and Business Directory
Caribbean Business Development Group
67 Wall Street, Suite 2411
New York, New York 10005
Ph (212) 323-7952
Fax (212) 432-9366

National Directory of Minority Owned Business Firms
Business Research Services, Inc.
4201 Connecticut Avenue NW, Suite 610
Washington, DC 20008
Ph (212) 364-6473
Fax (212) 686-3228

National Minority Chamber of Commerce
National Association of Black and
Minority Chamber of Commerce
117 Broadway
Oakland, California 94607-3715

Regional Directory of
Minority and Woman Owned Business Firms
Business Research Services, Inc.
4201 Connecticut Avenue NW
Washington, DC 20008
Ph (202) 364-6473
Fax (202) 686-3228

Roster of Minority Financial Institutions
United States Department of the Treasury
401 14th Street SW
Washngton, DC 20227
Ph (202) 874-6799

The Urban Banker
National Association of Urban Bankers
810 First Street NW, Suite 530
Washington, DC 20002
Ph (202) 783-4743

Who's Who of Black Millionaires
Who's Who of Black Millionaires, Inc.
P.O. Box 12092
Fresno, California 93776
Ph (209) 233-1346

Local Organizations

Alabama

Birmingham Minority Business Development Center
Suite 304
2100 16th Avenue
Birmingham, AL 35205
(205) 930-9254

Mobile Minority Business Center
Suite 102
801 Executive Park Drive
Mobile, AL 36606
(205) 471-5165

Montgomery Minority Business Development Center
Suite 209
770 South McDonough Street
Montgomery, AL 36104
(205) 834-7598

National Association of Minority Contractors
Alabama Chapter
401 Belt Line Drive
Mobile, AL 36617

National Black MBA Association
Birmingham Chapter
Post Office Box 370132
Birmingham, AL 35237
(205) 591-1200

Alaska

Alaska Minority Business Development Center
Suite 200
1577 C. Street Plaza
Anchorage, AK 99501
(907) 274-5400

Arizona

Phoenix Minority Business Center
Suite 210
1661 East Camelback
Phoenix, AZ 85016
(602) 277-7707

Tucson Minority Business Development
181 West Broadway
Tucson, AZ 85702
(602) 629-9744

Arkansas

Little Rock Minority Business Development Center
Suite 740
1 Riverfront Plaza
North Little Rock, AK 72114
(501) 372-7312

National Association of Minority Contractors
Arkansas Chapter
P.O. Box 5121
Little Rock, AK 72119
(501) 375-6262

California

Anaheim Minority Business Development Center
Suite 1050
6 Hutton Center Drive
Santa Ana, CA 92707
(714) 434-0444

Bakersfield Minority Business Development Center
218 South 8th Street
Bakersfield, CA 93304
(805) 837-0291

Black Business and Professional Association
119 East Eighth Street
Long Beach, CA 90813
(310) 499-1038

Business Equity and Development Project
Suite 200
1411 West Olympic Boulevard
Los Angeles, CA 90015
(213) 385-0351

Fresno Business Development Center
Suite 103
2010 North Fine
Fresno, CA 93727
(209) 252-7551

Golden State Business League
Suite 203
333 Hagenberger Road
Oakland, CA 94021
(414) 635-5900

Los Angeles Minority Business Development Center
Suite 700
3807 Wilshire Boulevard
Los Angeles, CA 90010
(213) 380-9471

National Black MBA Association
Los Angeles Chapter
P.O. Box 43009
Los Angeles, CA 90043
(213) 964-3053

National Black MBA Association
San Francisco Chapter
P.O. Box 3683
San Francisco, CA 94119-3683

Northern California Black Chamber of Commerce
5741 Telegraph Avenue
Oakland, CA 94609
(510) 464-8062

Oxnard Minority Business Center
451 W. 5th Street
Oxnard, CA 93030
(805) 483-1123

Riverside Minority Business Development Center
Suite F
1060 Cooley Drive
Cotton, CA 92334
(714) 824-9695

Sacramento Black Chamber of Commerce
1009 22nd Street
Sacramento, CA 95816
(916) 392-7222

Sacramento Minority Business Development Center
Suite C and D
630 Bercut Drive
Sacramento, CA 95814
(916) 443-0700

Salinas Minority Business Development Center
Suite B
123 Capital Street
Salinas, CA 93901
(408) 754-1061

San Francisco Black Chamber of Commerce
Suite 205
1426 Filmore Street
San Francisco, CA 94102
(415) 922-8720

San Francisco/Oakland Minority Business Development Center
1000 Broadway Suite 270
Oakland, CA 94607
(415) 465-6756

San Jose Minority Business Development Center
Suite 600
150 Almaden Boulevard
San Jose, CA 95150
(408) 275-9000

Santa Barbara Minority Business Development Center
Suite G
331 Milpast Street
Santa Barbara, CA 93103
(805) 965-2611

Stockton Minority Business Development Center
Suite F
5361 N. Pershing Avenue
Stockton, CA 95207
(209) 466-7222

Colorado

Colorado Black Chamber of Commerce
517 East 16th Avenue
Denver, Colorado 80205
(303) 832-2242

Denver Minority Business Development Center
4450 Morrison Road
Denver, CO 80219
(303) 937-1005

Connecticut

Connecticut Minority Business Development Center
410 Asylum Street
Hartford, CT 06103
(203) 246-5371

District of Columbia

District of Columbia Chamber of Commerce
1411 K Street
Washington, DC 20004
(202) 347-7202

Washington Minority Business Development Center
Suite 1120
1133- 15th Street NW
Washington, DC 20005
(202) 785-2886

Florida

Florida First Coast Chapter/ National Business League
8905 A Castle Boulevard
Jacksonville, FL 32208
(904) 765-2339

Jacksonville Minority Business Development Center
Suite 300
218 West Adams Street
Jacksonville, Florida 32202-3502
(904) 353-3826

Minority Women Business Enterprise
201 S. Rosalind Avenue
Orlando, FL 32801
(407) 836-7317

National Black MBA Association
South Florida Chapter
P.O. Box 694154
Miami, FL 33269-4154

National Business League
Tri County Chapter
P.O. Box 1626
West Palm Beach, FL 33402-1828
(407) 996-0465

Orlando Minority Business Development Center
Suite 211
32 E. Colonial Drive
Orlando, FL 32801

South Florida Business league
555 NE 15th No 31A
Miami, FL 33132

West Palm Beach Minority Business Development Center
Suite 301
2001 Broadway
Riviera Beach, FL 33404
(407) 863-0895

Georgia

Atlanta Business League
818 Washington Street
Atlanta, GA 30315
(404) 584-6126

Central Savannah River Area Business League
PO Box 1283
Augusta, GA 30903
(404) 722-0994

National Black MBA Association
Atlanta Chapter
PO Box 158
Atlanta, GA 30301

Savannah Minority Business Development Center
Suite 201
31 West Congress Street
Savannah, GA 31401
(912) 236-6706

Hawaii

Honolulu Minority Business Development Center
Suite 100
1132 Bishop Street
Honolulu, HI 96813
(808) 536-0066

Illinois

Cosmopolitan Chamber of Commerce
1326 S. Michigan Avenue
Chicago, IL 60605
(312) 786-0212

National Black MBA Association
Chicago Chapter
P.O. Box 8513
Chicago, IL 60680
(312) 236-4480

Indiana

Gary Minority Business Development Center
567 Broadway
Gary, IN 46402
(219) 883-5802

Indianapolis Minority Business Development Center
Suite 319
617 Indiana Avenue
Indianapolis, IN 46204
(317) 685-0055

National Black MBA Association
Indianapolis Chapter
PO Box 2325
Indianapolis, IN 46206-2325

Kansas

National Business League
Wichita Chapter
1125 East 13th Street
Wichita, Kansas 67214
(316) 686-4959

Louisiana

African Chamber of Commerce
3028 Gentilly Boulevard
New Orleans, LA 70122
(504) 948-9769

Baton Rouge Minority Business Development Center
Suite D
2036 Woodale Boulevard
Baton Rouge, LA 70806
(512) 476-9700

New Orleans Business League
107 Harbour Circle
New Orleans, LA 70126
(504) 246-1166

New Orleans Minority Development Center
1683 N. Claiborne
New Orleans, LA 70811
(504) 523-5400

Maryland

Business League of Baltimore
1831 W. N Avenue
Baltimore, MD 21217
(410) 728-1234

National Business League
Montgomery County Chapter
c/o CIS
Suite 301
8720 Georgia Avenue
Silver Spring, MD 209110
(301) 588- 2977

National Business League
Southern Maryland Chapter
9201 Basil Court, No. 115
Landover, Maryland 20785
(301) 772-3683

Massachusetts

Black Research Development Foundation
MBA Research Team
2000 Massachusetts Avenue
Cambridge, MA 02140

Boston Minority Development Center
985 Commonwealth
Boston, MA 02215
(617) 353-7060

National Black MBA Association
Boston Chapter
McCormack Station
PO Box 3709 JW
Boston, MA 02101

National Business League
Boston Chapter
500- 502A Harrison Avenue
Boston, MA 02118
(617) 247-9141

Michigan

Booker T. Washington Business Association
2885 E. Grande Boulevard
Detroit, MI 48202
(313) 875-4250

Detroit Minority Business Development Center
Suite 3701
65 Cadillac Square
Detroit, MI 48226-2822
(313) 961-2100

National Black MBA Association
Detroit Chapter
PO Box 02398
Detroit, MI 48202
(313) 972-4832

Minnesota

Minneapolis Minority Business Development Center
LL35
2021 East Hennepin Avenue
Minneapolis, MN 55413
(612) 378-0361

National MBA Association
Twin Cities Chapter
PO Box 2709
Minneapolis, MN 55402

Mississippi

Bureau of Business and Economic Research
Jackson State University School of Business
PO Box 18525
Jackson, MS 39203
(601) 968-2028

Jackson Minority Business Development Center
5285 Galaxie Drive
Jackson, MS 39206
(601) 362-2260

Natchez Business and Civic League
1044 N. Pine Street
Natchez, MS 39120
(601) 442-6644

Missouri

Black Economic League of Greater Kansas City
Suite 300
1610 E. 18th Street
Kansas City, MO 64108
(816) 474-1080

Kansas City Minority Business Development Center
Suite 1600
1101 Walnut Street
Kansas City, MO 64106
(816) 471-1520

Mound City Business League
10345 Nashua
Dellwood, MO 63136
(314) 361-2613

National Black MBA Association
Kansas City Chapter
PO Box 410692
Kansas City, MO 63115
(816) 822-7898

National Black MBA Association
St. Louis Chapter
PO Box 5296
St. Louis, MO 63115

St. Louis Minority Business Development Center
Suite 1200
500 Washington Avenue
St. Louis, MO 63101
(314) 621-6232

Nevada

Las Vegas Minority Business Development Center
Suite K
2860 E. Flamingo
Las Vegas, NV 89121
(702) 892-0151

Nevada Black Chamber of Commerce
1048 W. Owens
Las Vegas, NV 89106
(702) 648-6222

New Jersey

National Black MBA Association
Central New Jersey Chapter
PO Box 127
Piscataway, NJ 08854
(718) 479-4451

National Business League
South Jersey Chapter
PO Box 1382
Atlantic, NJ 08854
(908) 246-2878

National Minority Business Council
Suite 600
494 Broad Street
Newark, NJ 07102
(212) 573-2385

New Brunswick Minority Business Development Center
Room 102
134 New Street
New Brunswick, NJ 08901

New York Metropolitan Business League
Suite 200
20 N. Van Brunt
Englewood, NJ 07631
(201) 568-8145

Newark Minority Business Development Center
Room 102
134 New Street
Newark, NJ 07102
(201) 623-7712

New York

Association of Minority Business Enterprises of New York
Suite 3
165 40A Baiale Boulevard
Jamaica, NY 11434
(717) 341-0707

Bronx Minority Business Development Center
Suite 702
349 E. 149th Street
Bronx, NY 10451
(212) 665-8583

Brooklyn Minority Business Development Council
Room 1903
16 Court Street
Brooklyn, NY 11201
(718) 522-5880

Buffalo Minority Development Council
523 Delaware Avenue
Buffalo, NY 14202
(716) 885-0336

**Council of Economic Development
and Empowerment of Black People**
63 West 125th Street
New York, NY 10027
(212) 722-1922

Manhattan Minority Business Development Center
Suite 2212
51 Madison Avenue
New York, NY 10010
(212) 779-4360

**National Association of Negro Business &
Professional Women's Clubs**
Rochester Genesee Valley Club
49 Alden Road
Rochester, NY 14626
(716) 225-6771

National Black MBA Association
New York Chapter
Grand Central Station
Post Office Box 1602
Grand Central Station
New York, NY 10163
(212) 978-4333

Queens Minority Business Development Center
110-29 Horace Harding Expressway
Corona, NY 11368
(516) 484-9797

Rochester Minority Business Development Center
350 N Street
Rochester, NY 14605
(716) 232-6120

Uptown Chamber of Commerce
Suite 206
125th Street
New York, NY 10027
(212) 427-7200

Williamsburg/Brooklyn Minority Business
Development Council
12 Heywood Street
Brooklyn, NY 11211
(718) 522-5620

North Carolina

Carolinas Minority Supplier Developer Council
Suite 340
700 E. Stonewall Street
Charlotte, NC 28202
(704) 372-8731

Charlotte Minority Business Development Center
Suite 360
700 E. Stonewall Street
Charlotte, NC 28202
(704) 334-7522

Durham Business and Professional Chain
PO Box 1088
Durham, NC 27702
(919) 683-1047

Fayetteville Business and Professional Club
PO Box 1387
Fayetteville, NC 28302
(919) 483-6252

Fayetteville Business League
Fayetteville, NC 28301
(919) 483-6252

Fayetteville Minority Business Development Center
114 ½ Anderson Street
Fayetteville, NC 28302
(919) 483-7513

National Black MBA Association
Raleigh/Durham Chapter
PO Box 728
Durham, NC 27702
(919) 682-9690

Oxford Business and Professional Chain
PO Box 1553
Oxford, NC 27565
(919) 693-8874

**Raleigh/Durham Minority Business
Development Center**
Suite 8
817 Newbern Avenue
Raleigh, NC 27601
(919) 833-6122

Ohio

Black Economic Union of Ohio
10510 Park Lane Drive
Cleveland, Ohio 44106
(216) 231-0080

Cincinnati Minority Business Development Council
Suite 111
1821 Summit Road
Cincinnati, OH 45237-2810
(513) 679-6000

Cleveland Business League
2330 E. 79th Street
PO Box 99556
Cleveland, OH 44199

Cleveland Minority Business Development Council
Suite 335
601 Lakeside
Cleveland, OH 44114
(216) 664-4150

Council for Economic Opportunities in Greater Cleveland
668 Euclid Avenue
Cleveland, OH 44114
(216) 696-9077

National Black MBA Association
Cincinnati Chapter
PO Box 3391
Cincinnati, OH 45201
(513) 723-3448

National Black MBA Association
Cleveland Chapter
PO Box 22839
Beachwood, OH 44122

National Black MBA Association
Dayton Chapter
PO Box 5697
Dayton, OH 45405

National Business League
Stark County Chapter
Suite 3F
323 Salem Avenue
Canton, OH 44705
(216) 454-8081

Oklahoma

Tulsa Minority Business Development Center
240 E. Apache Street
Tulsa, OK 74106-3799
(918) 592-1995

Greenwood Chapter of Commerce
130 N. Greenwood Avenue
Tulsa, OK 74120
(918) 585-2084

National Business League
Oklahoma City Chapter
PO Box 11221
Oklahoma City, OK 73136
(405) 843-6400

Oregon

National Business League
Oregon Chapter
6431 Martin Luther King, Jr. Boulevard
Portland, OR 97211
(503) 260-9000

Pennsylvania

Business and Professional Association of Pittsburgh
4909 Pennsylvania Avenue
Pittsburgh, PA 15224
(412) 362-5702

National Black MBA Association
Philadelphia Chapter
PO Box 1384
Philadelphia, PA 19105
(215) 472-2622

National Black MBA Association
Pittsburgh Chapter
PO Box 3502
Pittsburgh, PA 15230
(412) 341-7452

Philadelphia Federation of Black Business and Professional Organizations
9200 Bustleton Avenue
2112 Lloyd Bldg.
Philadelphia, PA 19115

Philadelphia Minority Business Development Center
125 N. 8th Street, 4th Fl.
Philadelphia, PA 19106
(215) 629-9841

Pittsburgh Minority Business Development Center
9 Pkwy. Center, Suite 250
Pittsburgh, PA 15220
(412) 921-1155

South Carolina

Columbia Minority Business Development Center
2711 Middleburg Drive, Suite 114
Columbia, SC 29204
(803) 256-0528

Greenville/Spartanburg Minority Business Development Center
300 University Ridge, Suite 200
Greenville, SC 29601
(803) 271-8753

Tennessee

Black Business Association
555 Beale Street
Memphis, TN 38103
(901) 527-2222

Memphis Minority Business Development Center
5 North 3rd Street, Suite 2020
Memphis, TN 38103
(901) 527-2298

Nashville Minority Business Development Center
14 Academy Place, Suite 2
Nashville, TN 37210
(615) 255-0432

National Business League
Mid-South Chapter
918 South Pkwy., East
Memphis, TN 38106

Texas

Austin Minority Business Development Center
301 Congress Avenue, Suite 1020
Austin, TX 78701
(512) 476-9700

Beaumont Minority Business Development Center
550 Fannin, Suite 106A
Beaumont, TX 77701
(409) 835-1377

Brownsville Minority Development Center
3649 Leppard Street
Corpus Christi, TX 78408
(512) 887-7961

Capitol City Chamber of Commerce
5407 N. IH 35, Suite 304
Austin, TX 78723
(512) 459-1181

Dallas Black Chamber of Commerce
2838 Martin Luther King, Jr. Blvd
Dallas, TX 75215
(214) 421-5200

Dallas/Fort Worth Minority Business/Development Center
1445 Ross Avenue, Suite 800
Dallas, TX 75202
(214) 855-7373

El Paso Minority Business Development Center
1312-A E. Rio Grande Street
El Paso, TX 79902
(915) 544-2700

Fort Worth Metropolitan Black Chamber of Commerce
2914 E. Rosedale, Suite 101
Fort Worth, TX 76105
(817) 531-8510

Houston Minority Business Development Center
1200 Smith Street, Suite 2800
Houston, TX 77002
(713) 650-3831

Laredo Minority Business Development Center
2801 E. Montgomery, Suite 210
Laredo, TX 78043
(210) 725-5177

Lubbock/Midland-Odessa
Minority Business Development Center
1220 Broadway, Suite 509
Lubbock, TX 79401
(806) 762-6232

McAllen Minority Business Development Center
1701 W. Bus. Hwy. 83, Suite 306
McAllen, TX 78501
(512) 687-5224

Minority Business Association
625 E. 10th Street, Suite 800
Austin, TX 78701

National Black MBA Association
Dallas Chapter
PO Box 797174
Dallas, TX 75379
(214) 558-1699

National Black MBA Association
Houston Chapter
PO Box 56525
Houston, TX 77256

National Black League
Austin Cen-Tex Chapter
3724 Airport Blvd.
Austin, TX 78722
(512) 476-3506

National Business League
Dallas Chapter
PO Box 11331
Dallas, TX 75223
(214) 952-9959

Odessa Black Chamber of Commerce
700 N. Grant, Suite 200
Odessa, TX 79761
(915) 332-5812

San Antonio Minority Business Development Center
801 South Bowie
San Antonio, TX 78294
(512) 224-1945

Texarkana Black Chamber of Commerce
414 Texas Blvd.
Texarkana, TX 75501
(903) 792-8931

Utah

Salt Lake City Minority Business Development Center
350 East 500 South, Suite 101
Salt Lake City, UT 84111
(801) 328-8181

Virgin Islands

Virgin Islands Minority Business Development Center
81-AB Princess Gade
St. Thomas, VI 00804
(809) 774-7215

Virginia

Metropolitan Business League
121 E. Marshall Street
PO Box 26751
Richmond, VA 23261
(804) 649-7473

Newport News Minority Business Development Center
6060 Jefferson Avenue, Suite 6016
Newport News, VA 23605
(804) 245-8743

Norfolk Minority Business Development Center
355 Crawford Pkwy., Suite 608
Portsmouth, VA 23704
(804) 399-0888

Washington

Seattle Minority Business Development Center
155 NE 100th Avenue, Suite 401
Seattle, WA 98118
(206) 525-5617

Tacoma-Pierce County Business League
1321 South K Street
PO Box 5076
Tacoma, WA 98405
(206) 272-7498

Washington State Business League and Chamber of Commerce
PO Box 18528
Seattle, WA 98118
(206) 859-8284

Wisconsin

Milwaukee Minority Business Development Center
1442 N. Farwell Avenue, Suite 500
Milwaukee, WI 53202
(414) 289-3422

Milwaukee Minority Chamber of Commerce
2821 N. 4th Street, Suite 302
Milwaukee, WI 53212
(414) 264-4111